THE

DISSIDENT

REVIEW

Volume I

THE DISSIDENT REVIEW

VOLUME I

A Reclamation & Revitalization of the Past

FOREWORD

Today, the past is controlled by an academic elite which has abandoned its purpose — the search for truth, and the expansion of human knowledge. Instead, fanatics run our institutions of learning, and they have replaced truth with ideology. Dissent is not permitted in their journals.

The Dissident Review changes that. Our mission is to publish controversial, banned, and subversive historical research. We require no credentials and publish solely based on merit — because *self-education, led by love of what you study, is the only education that matters*. We aim to cultivate that education, and give a voice to the massive untapped talent that exists outside of academia.

The academic establishment has forbidden the pursuit of truth, deeming it offensive and dangerous. They fear it because history does not support their ideas. Their shallow perversions of the historical record crumble under the slightest scrutiny. Our goal is to rekindle the spirit of decades and centuries ago, with research not hindered by modern ideology. Merit will once again be able to speak for itself.

In short, we offer a voice to those who wish to challenge the mainstream. More specifically, the goal of this publication is to challenge the historical narratives that most people hold as truth — the ideas that cannot be questioned in the mainstream; the ideas that frame postmodern technocratic neoliberal democracy as the fulfillment of human destiny. History is everything in how one thinks about themselves and the world, and allowing it to be dominated by ideologues has been a disaster. People without an ounce of vitality or wisdom write our histories, and it shows in how most people think of the past. They think of it as a dark, unenlightened time; they think that it must be apologized for; they think that it must be abandoned.

But if dissenting ideas can reach the public square, this can be changed. Unfortunately, this cannot happen via traditional institutions; they are too far gone. Hence building an alternative institution, with a new model — and without the restrictions that plague mainstream publishing and academia.

Despite modern propaganda, we always want to learn more about the past. More importantly, we want to be inspired by it, and inspired by the spirit of discovery of it. Anything that feeds this innate desire can drastically alter one's self-perception and one's perception of the world — hopefully, for the better.

For this inaugural edition, we received excellent writing across time periods, fields, and interests, from writers of all backgrounds. What follows is a selection of the best, and the first in what will hopefully be a long tradition of inquiring about — and drawing inspiration from — parts of the past that the mainstream maligns or refuses to acknowledge. Thank you to all the writers who submitted their work, and thank you, reader, for your support.

TABLE OF CONTENTS

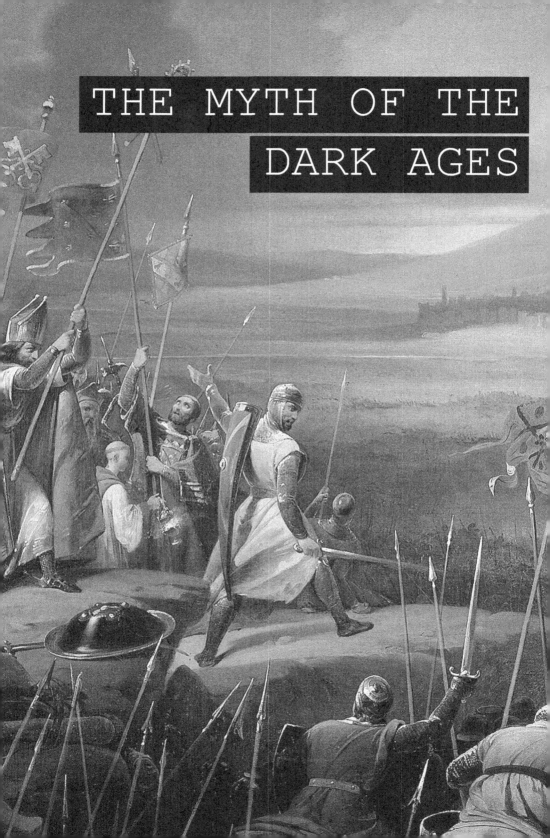

THE MYTH OF THE
DARK AGES

The Myth of the Dark Ages

By Alaric the Barbarian

I

Of all the grand historical narratives that have recently entered the political realm, the myth of medieval European "backwardness" and concurrent Islamic "progress" is perhaps the most egregious. The popular view of the Middle Ages holds that it was an era of immense suffering, religious fanaticism, oppression, and a time of cultural "backsliding", in that European society lost the virtues and advancements of Greek and Roman civilization. At best this is a misconception, and at worst it is a lie upheld for political purposes.

Broadly, our concept of the past has always been in flux, changing alongside contemporary ideas and influences. In some ways, the academic study of history is nothing but present-day politics applied to past events; historians and politicians alike take our ancestors and cram them into modern moral frameworks, hoping to advance whatever idea to which they are subscribed. Most often this involves the omission of contradictory information, but in some cases it's constructive—with the so-called Dark Ages, ideologues have built up a historical framework from pure subversion, aiming to create a founding mythos for postmodern materialist democracy. In fact, the "dark ages" interpretation is so counterfactual that it's dying in the scholarly world, even with its strong left-wing dogma.

Despite this, it remains at the forefront of modern political discourse. Further, the image of medieval Europe as dark, grimy, and barbaric is cemented in the cultural milieu through media depictions of the era. The notion is used in the West as a potent weapon to advance rootlessness, self-hatred, cultural decay, and moral relativism. In particular, the notion that European culture, scholarship, and technology was suppressed by the Church is treated as fact and used as a cudgel against Christianity and Western culture.

But it's simply untrue.

No foundation built on such blatant lies can last, and it is only the study of facts that can dispel weaponized slants about the past. So, let us examine the so-called "Dark Ages", and give the era an unbiased treatment, for which it is long overdue.

The myth of the "Christian Dark Ages" is not a new one. In fact, the term's first usage was during what is now thought of as the Dark Ages: in the early 14th century, Petrarch used the term to characterize scholarship in the post-Roman era. However, his usage of the terms "darkness" and "light" was far different from the modern connotation of peaceful, democratic progress vs. anti-intellectualism, barbarism, and decay. Rather, Petrarch used the traditional good-vs.-evil connotations of light and darkness to criticize the hubris of his age, and to oppose a contemporary form of historical revisionism—the notion that Greece and Rome were "dark" and therefore wicked due to their paganism. Rather, he lauded the cultural output of Antiquity, and cautioned contemporary scholars against discarding the achievements of the era. Essentially, he wanted scholars to avoid becoming so focused on the Current Thing of their era that they would disregard the expression of greatness found in Classical civilization.

Of course, this view is a world away from what we now think of regarding the "Dark Ages". Petrarch was commenting on the particularities of scholarship in his era; he wasn't claiming that Europe had fallen into disrepair and cultural backwardness due to the dominance of Christianity, which is the core tenet of the modern Dark Ages notion.

That insidious concept began later, during the Enlightenment. Secular philosophers of the era were the first to come to a now-common (though still equally ignorant) idea—that religion "holds society back" and "prevents progress". This argument made extensive use of slanted historical arguments, and in some cases blatant revision. In fact, the first treatment of history as a subject for philosophical analysis rather than narrative recording arose out of this goal, and has characterized the study of the past ever since.

The primary force behind this historiographical shift was Edward Gibbon, who argued that Christianity caused the fall of Rome. He denounced the following centuries as "a triumph of barbarism and religion"[1] — a truly Dark Age. Of course, it was his view that Roman social progress was reignited by the Renaissance and more importantly, the Enlightenment—a rather self-centered view. However, French philosophes picked up on these arguments, using them to support their arguments against Christianity, the Church, and more. A few examples:

"[After Rome fell], barbarism, superstition, and ignorance covered the face of the world." [2] – Voltaire

"Europe had relapsed into the barbarism of the earliest ages. ...[Europeans] lived some centuries ago in a condition worse than ignorance." [3] – Rousseau

Note that they considered religiosity and "ignorance" to be one in the same, not unlike modern atheists. They conveniently ignored the fact that the Roman state they idolized was staunchly religious, or that religious motives had driven much of the innovation, scholarship, and organization in their own society. Despite these obvious fallacies, this argument is co-opted today by atheists, leftists, and people who aim to destroy the idea of Western Civilization. They have even less nuance than the philosophes, and proclaim that the whole West was built on ignorance and barbarism. Their destructive goals all stem from their revulsion to Christianity, supported by this oversimplified, slanted theory of historical "progress".

Even outside of that anti-civilizational sect, we tend to lack a proper understanding of the European Middle Ages. As members of a secular Western culture, we find it difficult today to separate that secularization from our technological progress. We imagine that the progress we see today is exclusively the product of secularization, and lack a conceptual framework for a Western culture that advanced despite—or perhaps even due to—its religiosity. However, this seemingly contradictory society existed for centuries in Europe.

II

Despite the many polemics which have painted the Catholic Church as historically anti-science, the medieval era was a time of great technological and scientific advancement. The monastic tradition saw massive efforts undertaken to preserve, copy, and proliferate important manuscripts. Though many of the works of Plato and Aristotle were lost in the West, thousands of other important writings were painstakingly hand-copied and catalogued. New manuscripts were penned en masse, as well, including some of the foundational works of Christian philosophy (i.e. Aquinas' *Summa Theologica*) and massive poetic chronicles (i.e. *La Chanson de Roland*). In fact, our notion of a dearth of written literature in this era is mostly because much of it has been destroyed. However, catalogues like the recently-discovered Libro de los Epítomes (a catalogue of hundreds of lost books, collected and summarized by Christopher Columbus' son) give us tantalizing glimpses at a vast literary and philosophical tradition, reaching to the earliest days of the Middle Ages. This tradition included the writing and copying of religious works, philosophical treatises, fiction, poetry, geography, and work on the natural sciences. It must be restated that this work was undertaken in monasteries, under the direct supervision and control of the Church, supposedly the organization holding back the progression of knowledge. Monks were the primary scholars of the era, undertaking hundreds of experiments and observational studies. Consider the 12th-century monk Johannes de Sacrobosco, who in his work *Tractatus de Sphaera* accurately computed the size of the Earth by measuring the distance between the sun and the ground in two different cities. Many of these scientific inquiries arose out of monastic life and theological debate; for example, the problem of calculating the date of Easter catalyzed serious advancements in medieval astronomy. Further, the study of alchemy among monks and nobles led to the foundations of modern experimental chemistry, with extensive writing devoted to isolating elements and creating new compounds or metals. In fact, empirical science itself has its roots in medieval scholasticism, and names like Roger Bacon and Albertus Magnus are forever enshrined as pioneers of science. Admittedly, some sciences that had been pioneered in Greece and Rome were lost until the High Middle Ages—for example, early work on optics—but to say that the academic tradition died out in medieval Europe is to discredit the era's flourishing scientific and investigative tradition.

Additionally, to revisit the tired comparison of "advanced Islamic science vs. backwards European superstition", we must consider the differing concepts of education and study in each culture. Many point to the fact that the Islamic world built the first university as a demonstration of this point, but this ignores the differences between education between the cultures. Medieval European education was primarily tutor-based, and focused on practical matters—namely law and medicine. However, monasteries filled the role of modern university research departments; many great minds entered monastic life in order to devote themselves to study. The most extreme form of this devotion came in the form of cloisters—monks and nuns who were voluntarily sealed away in a small room, usually within a wall or tower. One such cloister was Hildegard von Bingen, who is singlehandedly responsible for writing over half of the surviving choral music from the era. She wasn't an oddity, either—hundreds of monks and nuns sealed themselves away, sometimes literally, to advance their chosen field. Again, this was not an age of intellectual repression by the Church—quite the opposite.

There is also the matter of technological progress, which was perhaps the strongest area of advancement in medieval Europe. This was immediately obvious in the area of transportation; as the scattered kingdoms of the post-Roman fallout became more interconnected, trade routes became increasingly complex, requiring better technology. Complex wagons and harnesses were invented, allowing for a thriving trade network across Europe (and indeed all the way to East Asia, via the Silk Road). Within Europe, roads were established and maintained along important trade routes—sometimes restored from earlier Roman projects, sometimes entirely new.

Additionally, oceangoing trade in the Mediterranean made Venice the "center of the world", and both shipbuilding and navigation technologies matured rapidly. Most notably, the compass and astrolabe entered common use, allowing for far more accurate navigation, and new methods of design and woodworking allowed for larger, faster ships. These industries advanced most particularly in Italy and Byzantium; shipbuilders and sailors from those regions were prized across both the European and Arab worlds. In fact, the navies of the Umayyad caliphate were built by imported Italian and Coptic shipwrights, manned by mercenaries from Byzantium or Egypt, and often captained by European naval commanders—all Christian.

Moreover, new inventions like the verge and foliot escapement mechanism (which allowed for the first true mechanical clocks) made commerce more efficient, and farming innovations (most notably the steel plow and the three-field system) allowed for vastly increased food production. These inventions, aimed at increasing efficiency and productivity, allowed for far greater per capita wealth and abundance, especially regarding food—meanwhile, the Arab world

7

remained stagnant in that regard. As a result, medieval Europeans were taller, heavier, and healthier than their Arab counterparts, a factor that would play into their military clashes alongside technological advancement. This abundance would also eventually allow for the vast military prowess and world-spanning empire that arose out of Europe, while the Islamic empires never expanded overseas.

This was a common thread across medieval European innovations—they were neither adopted nor matched in the Arab world. Most notably, as European transportation technology improved exponentially, the Islamic sultanates built no such infrastructure. From Rodney Stark: "Following the Muslim conquest of Egypt, the rest of North Africa, and Spain, the WHEEL disappeared from the whole area!" [4] The wheel disappeared because wheels required roads, and the Islamic world was not interested in building such infrastructure. True to their Bedouin roots, the Arab world would remain reliant on camels and walking for centuries.

III

The Islamic Golden Age was a time characterized by such contradictions. In fact, the term is as ambiguous and hotly-debated as the "dark ages" of Europe, but is generally agreed to have been a time between the 7th and 14th centuries, or some subset thereof—usually beginning with the reign of caliph Harun al-Rashid in 786. Islamic intellectual life in this time was rather centralized and well-financed, leading to many of the scientific and literary advancements for which it is now known today. Archiving older texts was a major profession, and innovations in mathematics, astronomy, medicine, and the natural sciences

8

abounded. Additionally, scholars argue that because the Eastern world had access to the works of the Greeks, they were able to "pick up where Aristotle and Plato left off" in developing a comprehensive natural philosophy. Scholars in Islamic courts were the first to identify the cranial nerves, had the first inklings of Darwinism, significantly developed algebra and trigonometry, accurately predicted the motion of celestial bodies, and more — this is all true.

But unlike the standard applied to Europe, the implicit argument made by those who vaunt these achievements is that devoutly religious Islamic governance led to this advancement. Quietly extended from this argument is the idea that Christianity is an anti-intellectual religion, whereas Islam is inherently friendly to scientific pursuits.

This notion couldn't be further from the truth. It is this specific notion — that Islamic religious predominance and governance allowed for a flourishing of intellectual culture, while the same circumstances in the Christian world led to intellectual decline – that is weaponized in modern discourse. The Islamic Golden Age of scientific discovery was certainly impressive, and a critical point in world history… but this was *despite* their religiosity, not because of it. Notably, Christian doctrine saw scientific study as a way to become closer in one's understanding of God, whereas Islamic dogma was far stricter — to Muslim theologians, one's understanding of the world should begin and end with the Quran. In fact, close study should more accurately frame the so-called "Islamic Golden Age" as the Near Eastern Golden Age, due to the diverse nature of the contributors, or perhaps even the Persian Golden Age, if we are to name it based on the group that made the largest single contribution.

9

Persian, Hindu, and Christian contributions to Islamic science are a touchy subject in Muslim scholarship, and as a result we in the West tend to get a watered-down picture of it. While the advances of the Islamic Golden Age were funded by Muslim caliphs and sultans, the actual scholars were more often Persian or Hindu dhimmis than Arab Muslims, and their study — particularly of astronomy — was more so a continuation of ancient Zoroastrian tradition than a new movement. Persian scholars "claimed" by the Arabs include al-Khwarizmi, father of algebra; al-Kashani, whose estimate of pi was unsurpassed for centuries; Rhazes, a pioneer of experimental medicine and the most prolific physician of his era; and the Banu Musa brothers, who produced important work on physics, engineering, and geometry, as well as inventing the first programmable machine (a type of automated flute).

Similarly eclipsed by the name "Islamic Golden Age" are the contributions of Christians, particularly Nestorians. Christian influence was most visible in the medical field and in translation work, but Christians worked broadly on intellectual pursuits, including theological writing and scientific research. In fact, the first center of Eastern thought in Late Antiquity were the (Christian) Academies at Nisibis and Gondishapur; this shifted to the Baghdad House of Wisdom under Muslim rule, but drew its traditions (particularly its system of medical training, including the first hospital systems and an early analogue to modern residency programs) from Gondishapur and the Christian scholars who built it. The result was a robust contribution to "Islamic learning" by Christian scholars.

This catalogue, of non-Islamic contributions to science claimed retrospectively by Muslim scholars, could be expanded over many more pages. The so-called Arabic numerals are really

Hindu, the geometrician and number theorist Thabit ibn Qurra was a pagan Sabian, Avicenna ("the most famous and influential of the philosopher-scientists of the Islamic world" [5]) was Persian, many leading engineers and shipwrights were Copts, and a massive portion of the vaunted translation work attributed to Arab scholars was actually undertaken by Christians and Jews.

Clearly, the story of the Islamic Golden Age is more complex than we have been led to believe, including major contributions from Persian, Christian, and Hindu scholars. But it isn't just the makeup of the scholars themselves that presents a complication in the narrative; the entire notion of Islamic leaders being friendly to science and scholarship is based on faulty assumptions.

In fact, beginning with Mutawakkil in 847, caliphs were actively hostile to science and research. In many cases, they suppressed such efforts by force, burning manuscripts and imprisoning scholars—the exact charges of anti-intellectual persecution typically levied at Christendom! After Mutawakkil, the astronomical research that continued was a far smaller, shadowy continuation of Zoroastrian and Nestorian traditions among the dhimmis, as anything that might contradict the Qur'an was taboo amongst the Muslim nobility and, if discovered, would be banned and destroyed. This is most famously exemplified in a certain anecdote regarding the Library of Alexandria, widely recorded in Islamic histories from the 9th century on. After the conquest of Alexandria in 641 AD, it was said that military commander Amr ibn al-As asked the caliph Umar what to do with the scrolls in the city's immense library, the largest in the ancient world. According to this account, 'Umar replied:

11

"If what is written in them agrees with the Book of God, then they are not required; if it disagrees, they are not desired. Therefore, destroy them." [6]

And thus, the Library of Alexandria was burned. According to the Islamic chronicler Abdul Latif, the paper was used as fuel to keep the bathhouses of Alexandria continuously lit for over six months. The veracity of this account is debated, and it is very likely untrue. However, its inclusion in so many proud Islamic histories, for centuries after the fact, demonstrates an important cultural norm—that this hostility to science was a point of pride in the Islamic world!

IV

Evidently, with any sort of in-depth study, the notion of a Christian "dark age" and a simultaneous Islamic "golden age" crumbles. However, as valuable as these cultural and intellectual comparisons are to understanding the differences between Islam and Christendom, there are more direct historical examples of comparisons between the cultures.

In fact, Islam and Christianity were quite deeply involved in a sort of comparison, throughout the medieval era and even into the Renaissance. They placed the best of their respective cultures against each other—people, technology, culture, and ideals—with nothing less than total annihilation on the line.

This is to say—they were engaged in war.

The armed conflict between Christendom and Islam was the longest war in human history. To see it as anything other than one, protracted conflict is to do it a disservice, to refuse to call it what it was: an existential struggle between the two religions. Beginning with the invasion of the Levant in 634 and ending with the Siege of Vienna in 1683, including conquests, reconquests, Crusades, jihad, piracy, and more, this war dwarfs all others in sheer scale.

Of course, it is necessary to examine this conflict if we are to evaluate the notion of "Islamic progress vs. Western backwardness" during the Middle Ages. The Iberian peninsula alone saw 760 years of brutal back-and-forth conquest, and the Crusades went off-and-on for two centuries. The Ottoman Empire extended to Vienna as late as the seventeenth century. To think of Western Christianity and Eastern Islam as two separate entities, or two divergent cultures uninterested in the affairs of the other, is ignorance. Rather, they were locked in a struggle of epic proportions for centuries, and this should inform our evaluation of the societal "merit" of each, if this is the frame to be applied to the period.

The first of these conflicts—the first jihad against Christians—was an invasion of the Holy Land itself. A mere two years after the death of Muhammad, the Rashidun Caliphate marched through Syria, burning churches and monasteries encountered along the way. In spite of modern secular revision, this was immediately seen as a religious war by combatants and leaders on both sides. Shouts of "Allahu Akbar" and "striking fear into the hearts of the infidels" abound in both Muslim and Christian chronicles, as do religious motifs and imagery—most particularly the imagery of the *houris* (women granted to jihadis in heaven) in Muslim chronicles. But the Christian Byzantines were no less fervent; during the Battle of Yarmuk, the right flank of the Byzantine formation—made up of particularly belligerent

Slavs—was said by Muslim chronicles to have bound themselves together with chains, and to have sworn on "Christ and the Cross and the Four Churches!"[7] to fight to the death.

Fight to the death, they did—the Muslims took the day, and rampaged on through the Levant and into Northern Africa. So began a centuries-long project of Islamic expansion into Christian lands, setting the stage for the civilizational clash between Europe and Asia Minor.

As the Islamic armies advanced to the east and north, only to be repelled at last by Constantinople herself, news of the brutal persecution of Christians in now-Muslim territories reached mainland European ears. Sensational accounts of Christians burned alive, nuns taken as concubines, and brutal tortures designed to force conversion were a topic of endless debate and condemnation in the Church and nobility (these accounts, by the way, were completely accurate, and enshrined "gloriously" in Muslim chronicles).

Soon, though, the threat would become much more tangible, as the Muslim empire began its invasion of the Iberian peninsula in 709, under Umayyad warlord Musa Bin Nusayr. After rampaging through modern-day Spain, "destroying on their way all the churches, and breaking all the bells",[8] Musa's forces were unimpressed by the military might of mainland Europe, and aimed to raze the land straight through to Constantinople. As they crossed the Pyrenees, the mood among the jihadis was triumphant; they had marched through a land of fractured leadership and poorly-organized Visigoth resistance, and their bags were already laden with spoils.

But they had not yet encountered a serious, organized force—not until they reached the heart of Gaul. With a massive

14

push of some 80,000 jihadi soldiers, none of whom had seen a single defeat in 20 years, the newest governor of the caliphate's European conquests—Abdul Rahman—pushed toward Tours, aiming to sack the Basilica of Saint Martin. On the Frankish side, Charles Martel's force lie waiting, though with vastly inferior numbers. After a week-long standoff in the woods of central France, the forces finally clashed.

It is in this battle that we see the first comparison of Western "backwardness" and Islamic "progress", in the winner-takes-all realm of warfare. The Muslim forces were made up near-entirely of light cavalry, "depending on bravery and religious fervor to make up for their lack of armor or archery."[9] Meanwhile, the Franks had developed and perfected a mixture of Roman and Gallic infantry tactics; they fought as a phalanx of heavy infantry, bearing massive interlocked shields interspersed with spears, and axes for both throwing and fighting. The Muslim forces relied on nomadic raider tactics and technology, outdated in Europe for centuries—dispersed cavalry charges aimed to break the enemy's ranks, then a slaughter as they routed. But Martel's men were cavalry-killers; already heavily armored, they formed human ramparts with their shields, relying on strict discipline and training to hold the line. When the Muslim horsemen tried their standard tactic—hitting the enemy line at a gallop and wreaking havoc within their ranks—they were unhorsed by a number of spears, then hacked and bashed to death with shields and axes. They simply couldn't break the shield wall of the Franks. The battle was a story of hundreds of these charges, each small and dispersed; every time, the Franks cut the riders down and advanced their line, never breaking their tight formation.

After a full day of bloody struggle, the armies returned to camp. When the Franks reformed in the morning, they discovered that what remained of the Umayyad army had fled. Estimates of losses differ between chroniclers and historians, but most agree that the Muslim forces took losses of at least 50%, and Franks less than 20%— an impressive feat for a force outnumbered at least 2:1. As a result, the Muslim horde was rapidly pushed out of Gaul, the extent of their conquest limited to Iberia—a foothold which would be chipped away over the seven centuries that followed. Martel's force, vastly outnumbered and fighting against an undefeated, widely-feared enemy, had in one battle halted the Islamization of Europe.

This battle echoes the story of almost every military contest between Islam and Christianity. For most of the Muslim imperial era, Eastern forces were consistently disorganized, self-interested, and fighting with technology and tactics that had long been outmoded in Europe. Meanwhile, European armies developed better technology, culminating in full plate armor, crossbows, and siege engines; as well as better tactics, which relied on group cohesion, the professionalization of fighting, and standardized equipment. Why was this?

In the period of strife after Western Rome fell, most of Europe was thrown into disarray as different groups rushed to fill the power vacuum. The entire continent waged war upon itself for nearly two centuries straight, with the only remaining semblance of central power in Rome unable to promote a unifying leader.

This meant that until (and during) the reign of Charlemagne, Europe served as a crucible: a testing-ground for military tactics and technology. The Early Middle Ages, or rather Late

Antiquity, was a time of iron sharpening iron, and military technology, logistics, and strategy advanced far faster in Europe than they did in the Near East. When an enemy in the East rose to challenge European territory, this well-honed war machine turned outward and repelled their clumsy attacks.

The bottom line is this: in martial matters, Christendom surpassed Islam, a disparity which never saw any serious efforts at rectification by Islamic empires. This fact is conveniently omitted by those who promote the idea of a "Christian dark age", not simply because it challenges the entire notion, but also because they are unwilling to accept the medieval era in Europe as being characterized by an existential threat from Islam. Also, many today are unwilling to accept martial excellence as an example of cultural advancement, even though it requires herculean feats of organization, production, and technological innovation.

This point is best exemplified by the Crusades, a time endlessly maligned by modern historians as an act of selfish Christian aggression against the peaceful, scientifically-minded Islamic caliphate. Evidently, the Crusades were not the "first act of aggression" between Islam and Christendom. However, there is something to be said about their methodology, and the success that they achieved.

While Muslim incursions into Europe resulted in nothing more than pillage and a "booty economy"—in that the invading force left a trail of nothing more than destruction, rape, forced converts, and pillaged churches—crusading knights engaged in state-building and the bolstering of city defenses. They were also hundreds of miles from support; indeed the wars for the Holy Land represent one of the earliest instances of a modern "foreign war", in that significant territory controlled by both the enemy and other interests lay between the conflict area and the home front. This required an incredibly sophisticated supply chain, and the fact that certain Crusader kingdoms lasted for over a century while surrounded by Muslim-controlled land is a testament to their technological and strategic merit.

The disparity between Christian and Muslim militaries and logistics was immediately obvious to the Muslims who tried to repel the First Crusade. The entire undertaking baffled Muslim soldiers and commanders—tens of thousands of knights and soldiers, from different Western kingdoms, setting off through southeastern Europe and Constantinople to invade the Holy Land. Despite taking heavy losses along the way, the crusaders passed through Constantinople and achieved a shaky initial success at Nicaea. They then advanced toward the ruins of Dorylaeum, which would be the first true test of crusader mettle against the full force of the Muslim Turks.

This battle began with a surprise attack by the Turks. Despite the 350-year span between the decisive clash at Tours and this attack, Muslim military tactics had changed little—they still fought as light, disorganized, sword- and bow-wielding cavalry. The situation on that day was quite similar to Tours, actually— the force disparity heavily favored the Muslims, a group led by Turkish prince Kilij Arslan, with its ranks bolstered by other Turks as well as Persian and Albanian mercenaries. But despite their numbers, their tactics were even further outmoded than those of the Umayyads; Christendom had greatly improved in warfighting capability since then. After initial losses due to the surprise attack, the crusader army under Bohemond fell into formation, and Bohemond ordered the heavily-armored knights to dismount and reinforce the shield wall. In an echo of Tours, the light Turkish cavalry could not break this line, despite many attempts. Meanwhile, the hardest-hitting element of the crusader army was allowed to assemble behind Bohemond's force: the heavy cavalry.

A mounted knight was a sight to behold, and a fearsome force on the battlefield—especially against an army unprepared for such a foe. Heavily armored, with a large, similarly-armored warhorse, knights were essentially juggernauts. They didn't use the hit-and-run raiding tactics of the Muslim light cavalry; rather, they rode in formation and attacked with heavy lances, swords, and maces. Critically, the invention of stirrups during the Middle Ages allowed for this amazing amount of force per horseman; additionally, a superior diet and full-time training made members of the knightly warrior caste much larger and more physically imposing than their Muslim counterparts, not to mention their huge, purpose-bred horses. With this fearsome charge, the tide of the battle quickly turned, and it became a rout. The crusader cavalry chased the fleeing Turks from the main force and past their camp for a full day, inflicting massive casualties and paving the way forward toward Jerusalem.

Despite much hardship, the crusaders continued this pattern on the road to Jerusalem, engaging in open battles and sieges until the Holy City finally fell in 1099. The city then remained a Christian kingdom until 1187, surrounded entirely by Muslim-controlled territory and far removed from direct European support. The knightly orders—the Templars, Knights Hospitaller, Teutonic Knights, and others—maintained the defense of Jerusalem and other so-called "crusader kingdoms" (or Outremer), successfully repelling forces ten times their size or more. They also dispatched knights with groups of pilgrims, who remained under constant threat of attack from Muslim bandits and raiders. In fact, thousands of pilgrims—including a vast number of peasants—made the trip to Jerusalem during this era, one of the earliest examples of broad at-will travel in the world. To maintain the security of this territory and passage, deep in the area controlled by enemies and without easy access to reinforcements, was a logistical and strategic feat unmatched in the Islamic world, and a testament to Christian advances in the fields of warfare and transportation, not to mention the economic excess required to make such a thing feasible.

V

It is clearly time to reconsider how we think about the Middle Ages, especially the tired and ahistorical comparison of "backwards Christendom vs. enlightened Islam". Under any scrutiny, the idea of Christian repression of innovation and technology is clearly disproven; in fact, it was during the so-called "dark ages" that European cultures developed the technology and organization used to cement their later worldwide dominance. Also, the Islamic Golden Age proves to be something of a misnomer—a majority of the most important scientific and literary achievements under the caliphates were actually completed by Persian, Hindu, and yes, even Christian scholars, though eternally remembered by their Arabic names.

Today, when historians and politicians parrot myths about Islamic scientific dominance and simultaneous European squalor, they unwittingly repeat centuries-old Muslim propaganda, which still finds direct support today in the many Islamic terror groups of the Middle East, most namely the so-called Islamic State. Ideologues use this distinction to further their anti-Western goals (usually some form of leftism), unknowingly using arguments from the first serious enemy of the modern West—Islam.

If we are to characterize the age with such a limited framework—a comparison of Christianity and Islam—it should be through the lens of the thousand-year military struggle between the two religions. Of course, in that case, the pertinent question is this: who won? The culture whose borders and political centralization constantly fractured and reshuffled, never reaching the heights of power and technological progress seen in Europe? Or the culture that expanded across the world, making English the default *lingua franca* of the world, and Christianity its predominant religion? When we consider the arc of history from the Middle Ages onward, the answer becomes clear. This life-and-death struggle, fought over a thousand years, should serve as a writ-in-blood reminder that the "dark ages" weren't quite so dark, and that Europe was no cultural backwater in comparison to the Near East—if that truly was the case, Islamic armies should have easily conquered it, and the Crusades would have been extinguished shortly after passing through Constantinople.

Often, when the "dark ages" myth is refuted in this manner, proponents will pretend that Islam and Christianity were never truly in an existential struggle, or that the Islamic world never had any interest in achieving dominance over Europe. They clearly forget the centuries-long struggle over Iberia, the battle of Tours, and most especially the Ottoman incursion into Europe as late as the 17th century. They certainly opt not to mention the heroic charge of the Polish winged hussars at Vienna in 1683—led by Polish king Sobieski himself—which once and for all repelled the Islamic threat, "striking fear into the hearts of the Turks and their Tartar allies." [10]

How we think about history is important, and the dark ages myth is a particularly critical element. If we believe that Western society and culture sprang from an impoverished age of ignorance and barbarism, how are we to take any pride in our principles, customs, or heritage? How are we supposed to appreciate and respect our historical roots, our cultural (and often literal) ancestors? Those who most strongly champion the idea of a Christian dark age in Europe understand the power of denying this pride, of bastardizing and subverting the past, and they take great delight in doing so. To let them win is a betrayal of one's identity and history.

In revisiting the Middle Ages, we must evaluate it as it was, from the few sources that remain. These may give a partial or incomplete vision, but the vision they present is one of prosperity, honor, vitality, heroism! In reading them, one sees that the Middle Ages in Europe were not characterized by some superstitious return to hovel-life, but rather a Promethean drive toward greatness and improvement, even—no, especially—in the face of existential threats. Far from an age of poverty—it was an age of vitality, of strength in the face of destruction! The best texts of the era read as exhortation; exhortation to strive for uncompromising morality, earthly greatness, and eternal remembrance, with no less clarity than Homer or Virgil. We must not abandon the spirit of the Middle Ages, relegating it in our minds to a long-past age of backwardness and gloom.

Instead, we must embrace it.

Endnotes

1. Gibbon, Edward. *The History of the Decline and Fall of the Roman Empire*, 1776-1788. Book 6, chapter 71.
2. Voltaire [François-Marie Arouet]. *Essai sur les mœurs et l'esprit des nations* [An Essay on Universal History, the Manners, and Spirit of Nations], 1756.
3. Rousseau, Jean-Jacques. Quoted in Peter Gay's *The Enlightenment*, 1966.
4. Stark, Rodney. *God's Battalions: The Case for the Crusades*, 2009, ch. 3.
5. Flannery, M. "Avicenna." *Encyclopedia Britannica*, December 23, 2022. Web.
6. Qifti, Ali ibn Yusuf. *T'arih al-Hukama*, tr. August Müller and Julius Lippert, 1903, p. 354-357. Edited for clarity.
7. Waqidi, Abu Abdullah Muhammad Ibn Omar al-. *Futuh al-Sham* [The Conquests/Openings of Syria], 1997, p. 194. Translated by Raymond Ibrahim in *Sword and Scimitar: Fourteen Centuries of War Between Islam and the West*, p. 24.
8. Maqqari, Ahmad ibn Muhammad. *The History of the Mohammedan Dynasties in Spain*, Vol. 1., 1999. Translated by Sir Gore Ouseley, p. 291. Quoted in Ibrahim, p. 75.
9. Davis, Paul K. *100 Decisive Battles: From Ancient Times to the Present*, 1999, p. 104. Quoted in Ibrahim, p. 81.
10. Thackeray, Frank W. et al., *Events that Formed the Modern World*, Vol. 1, eds. 2012, p. 268. Quoted in Ibrahim, p. 276.

Further Reading

God's Battalions: The Case for the Crusades by Rodney Stark

Sword and Scimitar: Fourteen Centuries of War Between Islam and the West by Raymond Ibrahim

The Devil's Broker: Seeking Gold, God, and Glory in Fourteenth-Century Italy by Frances Stonor Saunders

The English and Their History by Robert Tombs

The Light Ages: The Surprising Story of Medieval Science by Seb Falk

The Templars: The Rise and Spectacular Fall of God's Holy Warriors by Dan Jones

About the Author:

Alaric the Barbarian is the founder & editor of the Dissident Review. Aside from that, most other records have been lost to history.

Follow Alaric on Twitter: @0xAlaric

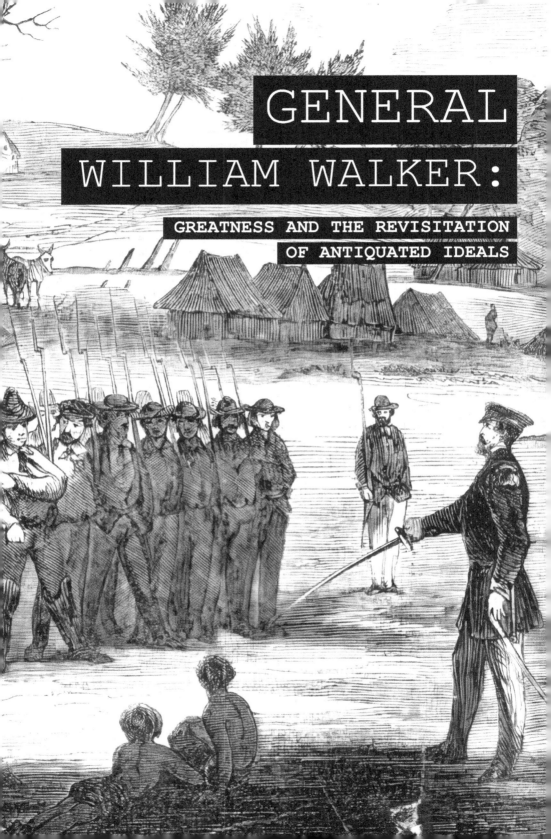

GENERAL WILLIAM WALKER:

GREATNESS AND THE REVISITATION OF ANTIQUATED IDEALS

General William Walker: Greatness and the Revisitation of Antiquated Ideals

By Anthony Bavaria

If you subscribe, even remotely, to the great man theory of history, then you cede to the basic fact of a hierarchy amongst men. Not all of humankind has equal potential; yes, trends and forces aid in elevating certain types of men that are ripe for the occasion, but this truism still speaks to the notion that we are different from each other. We've all seen the memes of a burly man that would have once been at the head of some crew of pagan marauders now relegated to a cubicle. Conversely, personalities that were probably once candidates to be eunuchs in the queen's chambers are now running society. This leads to an understanding that not all men destined for greatness necessarily succeed. Many try and fail, and though their greatness may not have impacted history in a meaningful, long-term way, their cause and effort are no less worth celebrating. One such man was William Walker and his enterprise was filibustering.

The act of droning at a governmental pulpit on behalf of some boring legislature is not what is being examined. Walker was involved with the antiquated, militaristic version of filibustering, also known as freebooting, which is broadly defined as a private individual raising funds and an army to engage in an unauthorized incursion into a foreign country. The goal of something like this can be broad, and the definition immediately likens this act to a plethora of similar activities such as proxy warfare, piracy, the employment of mercenaries, or government-aided coups. What separates freebooting from these other modes of combat is the ideology, relative autonomy, and goals of the filibuster. Today, few ideas are worth fighting for; in this essay, the cause of civilizational greatness and William Walker's attempt in spreading it by force will be examined.

Before the adventures of Walker can be fully analyzed, it must first be framed in the context of his impressive background. In *Filibusters and financiers; the story of William Walker and his associates*, author William Scroggs states that Walker's origins are "somewhat fragmentary." However, we do know that he was born in 1824 to Mary Norvell, daughter of a pre-revolutionary Virginia family of English heritage, and James Walker, listed only as "a Scotchman who settled in Nashville, Tennessee, in 1820." [1] Based on William's father's Scottish ancestry and his settling in Tennessee, there's a decent chance he's of some relation to the storied Walker family of American pioneering lore.

Looking for ways to tame all points of the North American continent west of the Appalachians, early American statesmen were at a loss. Large standing armies were currently out-of-vogue for the new nation that just fought against such practices, so they had to get creative in their conquering; demographic warfare proved to be a viable option. Initially courting lowland German migrants for their can-do, industrious attitudes, our founding fathers were dismayed when, upon their arrival, the Germans looked toward the mountains in the west, shrugged their shoulders, and decided to homestead in the old lands of William Penn; the direct descendants of these settlers are the Pennsylvania Dutch, Amish, and Mennonites. The second pick of the nation's early ruling class were their old cousins, the Ulster Scots, from which the Walker clan hailed. A people ripped from their homeland in northern England/lower Scotland for colonization efforts in Ireland, they were downtrodden, miserable, and forever yearning for a place of their own. Incentivized with these exact prospects in the new world, the Ulster Scots were shown the east-facing foothills of the Appalachian Mountains and officially unleashed.[2] Referred to as Scotch-Irish in the U.S., like wildfire they spread clear across the continent and finally achieved their place in the sun. One became president (Andrew Jackson) and another blazed some of the first overland routes to the Pacific (Joseph Walker).

An early Walker settlement was Tennessee. Hailing from Nashville, William was born late in the game, and by the time he was a young man—having successfully practiced medicine, law, and journalism all by the time he was twenty—most of the continent had been tamed; drunk on the idea of Manifest Destiny, however, the young man's ambitious were yet to be thwarted.

Now living in San Francisco, Walker was employed as a newspaper writer. When he wasn't pissing people off and engaging in pistol duels—he was in three and wounded twice, once by infamous wild west gunslinger William Hicks Graham—Walker was dreaming. His most grandiose idea was conquering lands to the south of the U.S. to form new "slave states" as buffer zones between America and what lay beyond. Though this sounds absurd, in the context of the era, it seemed within reach of any man that simply put his mind to it. Walker's kin had just recently taken a continent from wild savages, and his nation invented the locomotive and laid tracks from ocean to ocean... why wouldn't he be able to take what he saw as rightfully his? A Frenchman, Charles René Gaston Gustave de Raousset-Boulbon had just recently tried it in the Mexican region of Sonora, and now it was Walker's turn. Recruiting piss-and-vinegar men from his native Tennessee and neighboring states, Walker built his army. To finance the expedition, he sold scrips that would be redeemable in his newly established state of Sonora after its conquest.

When taking the fundraising efforts into consideration, a contemporary reader can easily deduce motives of personal financial gain from Walker's venture. The earlier mentioned concepts of piracy and guns-for-hire offer easy comparisons. However, the role of a mercenary is simply to make money and the endgame for a pirate is merely to steal booty; throughout history, few in these roles ever possessed illusions of state-building. In fact, the only community pirates and soldiers of fortune have ever created were usually intentionally devoid of any of the foundations of structured society, since scruples would only impede their wealth-attaining efforts.

Walker's first foray southward began in 1853. Leading a small army of only 45 men with himself as their Colonel, he invaded Baja California and captured the local governor. Lowering the Mexican flag in the region's capital of La Paz, Walker and his army raised their own. He unofficially claimed his conquered land as The Republic of Baja California, with himself as President. Further success was achieved when a Colonel in the Mexican Army came to replace the now captured governor; he too was taken into custody by the filibusters. Enticed by initial success, without having moved off the Baja peninsula, the Colonel preemptively added the land east of the Gulf of California to his newly named "Republic of Sonora." Cabling his exploits and new claims back to the U.S. had the benefit of attracting new recruits to the cause; roughly 200 additional men made their way south.

Unfortunately, a lack of supplies and increasing resistance from the Mexican Army forced Walker to retreat and ultimately abandon his newly acquired state. Now back in the U.S., the self-appointed Colonel was put on trial for breaking the Neutrality Act of 1794. This presents another opportunity to dispel any notions that he was acting on behalf of third party or financial interests. If the U.S. government was interested in furthering their control southward, they would have been aiding Walker, not putting him on trial. Washington had just recently finished a war with Mexico in 1848, and clearly wanted to avoid further conflict rather than stoke it in a way they would become skilled at, time and time again, in the following century.

As it is with most times throughout Western history, there was a massive disconnect between the people and their rulers. Though he was tried for treason, Walker's jury unanimously motioned for acquittal; he was a hero, not a villain. In *Mercenaries: A Guide to Private Armies and Private Military Companies*, author Alan Axelrod states, "Without question, he was guilty, but in an era when national expansion was overwhelmingly popular both in the South and in the West, no jury would convict him. After retiring for a mere eight minutes of deliberation, the jurymen returned with a verdict of not guilty." [3]

Undeterred, his sights were now set on Nicaragua. Civil war had erupted in the Central American country, and Walker sought to exploit. Allying himself with the Democratic Party against the Legitimists, Walker convinced the Democratic President to grant him and his freebooters the status of "colonists" (to avoid again violating the Neutrality Act) with an additional clause that they had a right to bear arms in service of the government. He and 60 men landed on the shores of their Central American target, received reinforcements of local troops, and quickly sought out action against Legitimist forces. The Battle of Rivas ensued; on the action, Scroggs states, "Rivas was attacked at noon on the 29th. Walker's native troops fled at the first fire, leaving his fifty-five Americans opposed to a force of over five hundred. The falanginos (a Spanish term derived from what Walker called his men: The American Phalanx) took refuge in several houses, where they were surrounded by the enemy and held at bay for four hours." [4] Though the filibusters ultimately withdrew from the town – they were outnumbered 6:1 – they inflicted disproportionately heavy casualties on their foe, killing 70 while only losing 11 of their own.

It's worth noting that by no means was Walker a rearguard leader. At another encounter, the Battle of La Virgin, the freebooter leader was grazed in the neck and also shot in the chest; the only reason he survived was the bullet luckily passing through a series of folded papers in his breast pocket. Again outnumbered almost 6:1, Walker and his men inflicted heavy losses, killing 60 while losing only two native fighters. Victorious at La Virgen, the army proceeded to Granada where he took control. Initially via a provisional president, Walker, now a self-styled General, was in command of Nicaragua. On 20 May 1856, American President Franklin Pierce officially recognized Walker's regime.

Partly because of his brash, courageous style of leadership, it should be no surprise that Walker's filibuster army attracted quite the array of wild men. Backgrounds of soldiers and supporters alike varied wildly: "Charles Frederick Henningsen, the European soldier of fortune, Domingo de Goicouria, the Cuban "liberator," Bruno von Natzmer, a Prussian cavalry officer, Frank Anderson, of New York, and Charles W. Doubleday, of Ohio; when he was induced to go to Nicaragua by Byron Cole, a New Englander; and when his enterprise was first chronicled and he himself greatly lauded by another New Englander, William V. Wells, a grandson of Samuel Adams." [5]

Sadly, this is where the waters become muddied; outside interests began to apply their weight. Going behind the big man's back, two underlings (C. K. Garrison and Charles Morgan) of railroad and shipping magnate Cornelius Vanderbilt underwrote Walker's expedition under the pretext he would seize Vanderbilt's steamboats that serviced the shipping lanes of Lake Nicaragua (a major pre-Panama Canal shipping route) and hand them over to the conspirators. Vanderbilt discovered the plot and immediately dispatched spies to neighboring Central American states to rouse support for a war against General Walker. Eventually, Costa Rica, Honduras, El Salvador, and factions within Nicaragua would all join together and take up arms against Walker's regime. Within two years, a series of battles and defeats culminated in the end of the freebooter state. On 1 May 1857, the General surrendered, indicatively, to a U.S. Navy Commodore. Though his native country's military took him away from his hard-won state, he was repatriated, of all places, to New York City, where he was greeted by the people as a hero.

After writing a book on his exploits, forever undeterred, Walker returned to Central America. With rumblings of a new filibuster crusade, annoyed British authorities—who had financial interests in the area—took him to a Royal Navy ship and put him under arrest. Rather than sending him home, the British naval officer in charge handed Walker over to the Hondurans, who promptly executed him by firing squad.

In addition to this man's entire life, what's amazing is the fact that established history on the saga openly admits "Because of this act (Walker seizing Vanderbilt's steamships), and others of a similar nature, revolts began to break out, fostered by Commodore Vanderbilt... Costa Rica declared war against him (Walker)." [6] Histories sympathetic to the Central American perspective on the subject love big business intervention here, but bemoan it in the following century. This basic fact, coupled with the British role of arresting Walker for fear of associated financial detriments clearly indicates that the money changers—the same groups that would soon be instigating coups in Central America and elsewhere throughout the globe via governmental agencies—were a direct impediment to the establishment of a grandiose ideal, where open martial prowess and the cementing of a way of life took priority. This competing-motives sentiment is best summarized by Brigadier General Smedley Butler:

"I helped make Mexico... safe for American oil interests in 1914. I helped make Haiti and Cuba a decent place for the National City Bank boys to collect revenues in. I helped in the raping of half a dozen Central American republics for the benefits of Wall Street. The record of racketeering is long. I helped purify Nicaragua for the international banking house for the Brown Brothers in 1909-1912. I brought light to the Dominican Republic for American sugar interests in 1916..." [7]

And the list goes on. With the above-mentioned oligarchical mindset becoming the prevailing one, it's no surprise that modern depictions of Walker, or men of his ilk, are overwhelmingly negative. It makes obvious sense that he'd be portrayed in a bad light in places like Nicaragua and Mexico; paintings of him losing battles abound, and there's even a giant statue of him sheepishly fleeing in Costa Rica. The truly depressing realization is that his legacy is equally besmirched in his home civilization. Brady Harrison's excellent book *Agent of Empire: William Walker and the Imperial Self in American Literature* actually catalogs all media that portrays Walker, directly or indirectly. The most absurd might be Alex Cox's film *Walker*. Known for his safe-edgy, art-house critique of Reaganism and other Conservative Inc. ideals (*Repo Man* is his most well-known), Cox intentionally presents silly depictions of militarism, to include tanks and helicopters, in his 1850's set movie about Walker. This is exemplified when Harrison states that Cox and others "dive into the darkest currents in American culture and represent imperialism as a spiritually and ethically twisted and deforming process." [8] When contemporary representations of Walker are juxtaposed to the opinions of him from *his* era, its clear things have changed. The best summary of the man comes from one of his officers that fought alongside him:

> "I do not wish to be understood as expressing the belief that General Walker in all things was a model of infallible wisdom. Like all of us, he was only human, and subject to errors of judgment as are other men… His unconquerable, yet calm courage; his contempt of danger; his exalted moral and intellectual character, and his supreme detestation of everything low or mean, are traits that won for him the respect and admiration of honest and sincere hearts that at the same time may have withheld approval of his purposes." [9]

Though Walker's type is a rarity, he wasn't alone in his quest for greatness. Nearly 70 years later, another exceptional man took on a comparable initiative. Upset with Italy's outcome in the aftermath of the Great War, poet Gabriele D'Annunzio spearheaded a new movement of ultranationalism. His cause had an eerie likeness to Walker's idea of American nationalism, and his goal—forcefully taking a city with armed troops not in a time of war—was similar to Walker's Central American freebooting. On 12 September 1919, D'Annunzio marched 2,000 Great War veterans and irregular soldiers into the Adriatic city of Fiume and declared it the Italian Regency of Carnaro; obviously, he claimed the title of "duce" for himself. Just like Walker, this was not for money or ulterior third-party motives, it was for the glory of himself and his people.

William Walker wasn't delusional; he was merely a great man at the end of a great age and the beginning of a terrible one. In a way, he was the inverse of what Michel Houellebecq refers to as "precursors" in *The Elementary Particles*; he states, "Well adapted to their time and way of life on the one hand, they are anxious, on the other hand, to surpass them by adopting new customs, or proselytizing ideas still regarded as marginal." [10] How on earth could Walker have known that Manifest Destiny wasn't an ever-growing idea for the average Westerner to stake his claim, but was now exclusively the privilege of financiers, mega corporations, and governments? Even Harrison admits, "What the filibusters sought in the 1850s… the White House and Congress were able to achieve on a much grander scale in the 1890s." [11] They even stole the term; the modern-day usage of the word filibustering being associated with the boring, running-out-the-clock technicality of killing a piece of legislature was somehow retconned from bold men invading entire countries on their own initiative. Maybe Walker was doomed to fail, one of Savitri Devi's men against time. Is standing defiantly against the tide an act, in and of itself, worth celebrating? According to the heroes of our civilization's lore—yes, it is.

Luckily, some influential people are sounding the alarm for a return to these seemingly extinguished attitudes. *Bronze Age Mindset* has much to say on the subject. Regarding our ancients: "The modern world is a killjoy, in short. But the ancient Greeks were quite different… What they admired was a carelessness and freedom from constraint that would shock us, and that upsets especially the dour leftist and the conservative role-player."[12] This is coupled with the idea of, "The free man is a warrior, and only a man of war is a real man." [13]

These quotes are highlighted without suggesting that the reader necessarily needs to form his own army and invade their neighboring country, however, it brings to mind the idea of the reclamation of space, of which much has been written about in dissident spheres. Though a lengthy summarization of mental and ideological space as well as physical—ranging from cities, forests, to average hang-outs—can be undertaken here, it's best to leave the interpretation up to the reader, with the emphasis of using the story of Colonel/General/President of Nicaragua William Walker as inspiration. In his book, *The War in Nicaragua*, Walker begins with the following dedication:

To My Comrades in Nicaragua

I dedicate this effort to do justice to their acts and motives: To the living, with the hope that we may soon meet again on the soil for which we have suffered more than the pangs of death—the reproaches of a people for whose welfare we stood ready to die: To the memory of those who perished in the struggle, with the vow that as long as life lasts no peace shall remain with the foes who libel their names and strive to tear away the laurel which hangs over their graves. [14]

Endnotes

1. Scroggs, William. *Filibusters and financiers; the story of William Walker and his associates*. (New York: The Macmillan Company), 1916, p. 9.
2. Gilbert, Bil. *Westering Man: The Life of Joseph Walker*. (Norman, OK: University of Oklahoma Press), 1985, p. 13-24.
3. Axelrod, Alan. *Mercenaries: A Guide to Private Armies and Private Military Companies*. (Washington, D.C: CQ Press), 2013.
4. Scroggs, William. *Filibusters and financiers; the story of William Walker and his associates*. (New York: The Macmillan Company), 1916, p. 109.
5. Ibid., 7-8.
6. Juda, Fanny. "William Walker." *The Museum of the City of San Francisco*.
7. Butler, Smedley & Parfrey, Adam (Introduction). *War Is A Racket: The Antiwar Classic By America's Most Decorated Soldier*. (New York: Feral House), 2003, p. 10.
8. Harrison, Brady. *William Walker and the Imperial Self in American Literature*. (Athens, GA: University of Georgia Press), 2004, p. 171.
9. Jamison, James. *With Walker in Nicaragua or Reminisces of an Officer in the American Phalanx*. (Columbia, MO: E. W. Stephens Publishing Company) 1909, p. 162.
10. Houellebecq, Michel. *The Elementary Particles*. (New York: Vintage International), 2001, p. 20.
11. Harrison, Brady. *William Walker and the Imperial Self in American Literature*. (Athens, GA: University of Georgia Press), 2004, p. 191.
12. Bronze Age Pervert. *Bronze Age Mindset*. 2018, p. 117.
13. Ibid., 112.
14. Walker, William. *The War in Nicaragua*. (New York: S.H. Goetzel & Co.), 1860.

About the Author:

Anthony Bavaria is a dissent writer. His work can be found in Man's World, Counter-Currents, and CovertAction Magazine. His interests lie at the intersection of culture, geo-politics, and history.

HISTORY
IS EVER
IN A
FLUX

History is Ever in a Flux

By Tozara Ayomikun

You may not know it, but you're living in one of the most unstable periods in recent history. The world has not seen this level of disturbance, chaos and uncertainty since the collapse of communism in 1989. The trajectory of the human future that seemed so certain to many of the world's leading political theorists 30 years ago is now muddled up and confused. You and I may be living through a transformation in the world order, and it shouldn't be any surprise if it doesn't seem like it to many, because the people living through a revolution almost never realize it, and individuals experiencing a historic moment almost never notice its significance. It usually takes the hindsight of future generations, who, having a more comprehensive and an outside view of events, are able to fully appreciate the true extent of the process.

In 1992, following the fall of the Berlin Wall which marked the end of the Cold War and the emergence of the United States as the world's preeminent nation, Francis Fukuyama published *The End of History and the Last Man*. As you can already infer from the title, it was an acknowledgement of a perceived finality, a statement of Fukuyama's conviction—even certainty—that human political evolution had come to an end. Whether this conclusion was justified based on the evidence of the time is contestable, but there can be little doubt that it was totally understandable. The victory of democracy over despotism, capitalism over communism, liberal democracy over fascism, and the institution of a new and unipolar world order under the aegis of American hegemony did give the impression that a final answer had been reached, that the End of History had indeed arrived.

Fukuyama's analysis was made from a theoretical perspective that finds its origins in Whiggish notions of history. Whiggish history views history as a linear process, always going from a more primitive stage to a more advanced one, from lower development to higher development, from an inferior stage to a superior stage. In this view, history has an end point towards which it is always progressing, and the present is always better than the past and the future always better than the present. It is the antithesis of age-old notions of "Golden Ages." It automatically antagonizes theories of degeneration, decadence and regression. Instead of looking to a once Golden era from which the human race had fallen, it anticipates a glorious future towards which humanity is accelerating. Fukuyama, seeing the victory of "freedom" in 1989 and the rise of a liberal world order that he was totally convinced would no doubt be the ultimate desire of all humans all over the world, concluded that this future "Golden Age" had been reached. A total error, as we shall see.

Of course, it wasn't only Fukuyama and his Whig predecessors who promoted this view of history. His more immediate influences, Georg Wilhelm Friedrich Hegel and Karl Marx, built their entire philosophical edifices on this theory. Hegel believed that history was a process moving towards a specific direction—

human freedom was its ultimate end, although he meant "freedom" in a metaphysical, idealist and "spiritual" sense that we do not have the time and space to elaborate on here. He wrote, "history is the process whereby the spirit discovers itself and its own concept." We can oversimplify that as "history is the culmination of consciousness," if that would help (I doubt it would, but we can't dwell on Hegel).

Marx turned Hegel's theory into a tool for economic analysis, and thus came up with his theory of historical and dialectical materialism, which got rid of the metaphysical connotations of Hegel's system while retaining its "arrow of history" — except that this time around the arrow was not about the progress and ascent of "the spirit" (whatever that is), but the evolution of man's material condition and its ultimate endpoint. In this Marxist history, material and economic forces are the driving engines, and progress is expressed in five stages. History begins as primitive communism, develops into slave society which eventually gives way to feudalism, feudalism then gives way to capitalism, which in turn evolves into socialism, and socialism culminates in a global, stateless communism. Stateless communism is therefore Marx's own End of History.

In 1989, the USSR collapsed, the capitalist West won the Cold War, thus denying global communism its expected take off. Socialism has been a massive failure wherever it has been tried, and in nations where socialist policies are partially implemented (such as the welfare state, free education, and free healthcare), it is always as an appendage of successful market capitalism, not its replacement. Marx's End of History is therefore nowhere in sight, and his prediction that capitalism would destroy itself with its internal contradictions and that the first Proletariat Revolutions would take place in the world's most capitalist countries

(America) have been utterly smashed into smithereens by the events of the 20th century. Rather, it was the USSR that was destroyed by its internal contradictions. What we have now is global capitalism. It was the liberal world order that triumphed, after all.

But does that mean the liberal world order was the *actual* end of history as Fukuyama believed? Does that mean America's unipolar world (an aberration of history) was a permanent feature—a final conclusion? Does that mean liberal democracy is the ultimate system of them all? One only needs to look around oneself and wonder what Fukuyama must be saying now. China and Russia have resisted the absorption of liberal democracy. The Islamic world remains antagonistic to the values of liberal democracy. All American attempts to bring "freedom and democracy" to the Middle East have been utter failures and embarrassments. Every single experiment has proven itself to be totally different from Germany and Japan. In Europe, Samuel P. Huntington's Clash of Civilizations is ongoing. Xenophobic sentiments are on the rise among the majority of American conservatives. Nationalism, Fascism, and Traditionalism are on the rise among some American and European youths.

America's unipolar world order is collapsing as it explodes abroad and implodes at home. The empire is tired and its dying ember is all we can see. And it looks like it will be dying with a whimper, not a bang. Sectarianism is tearing it apart. Its people have become so politically polarized that the rule of law is increasingly disrespected whenever it threatens ideological solidarity. Policy debates are becoming impossible to resolve with civility. Love for the nation is at an all time low. The Governor of California, the world's fifth largest economy and the biggest section of the American union, is giving secessionist signals. The Southern States want back segregation. Love for the Confederacy is resurfacing. Hispanics in Texas are pumped up for a breakaway. There is a full blown culture war where both sides feel deep hatred for the other and are intent on obliterating one another. The European front of the Empire is in chaos and the war in Ukraine has exposed the fragility of the EU. The Pacific front is also unstable, and there's a threat of a hyperpower on the horizon. The President of the Empire has been put in a position where he is forced to speak of World War III so casually.

What we're seeing before us is the victory of liberal democracy gradually receding, America's unipolar world slowly crumbling with a group of neocons in the Pentagon and the White House (who never believed that their unipolar victory was a guarantee that didn't need desperate measures to be preserved as Fukuyama theorized) talking about potential armed conflicts with Russia and China, refusing to fully accept that Fukuyama was completely wrong, that history never ended, that a multipolar world is inevitable, and that the last thirty years in the whole of human history have been just as fragile as they were unique.

The United States wants to maintain its hegemony at all costs, but it's already clear that this is impossible. It has two options: it starts an armed conflict with China and Russia and wreaks utter devastation on the world, or realizes that its near-peers are becoming actual peers and accepts the relegation of its hegemony to the Western Hemisphere, as was the case before the terrain-changing global wars of the last century. Either way, this would have significant transformative consequences for the world. It would see the end of some old alliances and the creation of some new ones. It would see the creation of new economic power blocs and the dissolution of some old ones. The end of America's world policing will definitely see the resumption of major wars in certain parts of the world, where conflicts have been quietly smoldering for decades but kept under wraps by the deterring posture of the United States. It would be a sweeping change that would have many unforeseen ripple effects as well. A consequential rearrangement that would no doubt have huge impacts that can only be fully appreciated decades after the fact.

It is important to state explicitly that all theories of human history that put impersonal forces at the center of the process of historical change are completely and utterly wrong. There are indeed forces that shape history, but these forces are not impersonal, nor do they act on passive human agents to bring about inevitable results. History is a product of interactions between human agents and their environments, because human agents are both active and reactive. The phenomenon of history finds explanation in man's responses to external stimuli and circumstances, as dictated by his biological nature. Greed, arrogance, quest for survival, quest for glory, security, respect for the sacred (in the form of religion and ancestral tradition, and so on). It is also important to keep in mind that the causal forces behind historical events can also originate entirely from the internal imagination of human agents, totally uninfluenced by external circumstances or considerations. We see this in the triumph of insane ideas that had no connection with reality — because they originated in the minds of individuals with typically psychiatric symptoms — but went on to significantly impact the evolution of society and change history anyway.

Political revolutions are often the result of the actions of a group of humans devoting themselves religiously to some random ideal and striving towards its realization, or human groups reacting to some external accident or circumstance. History is a chaotic mess. Nazism was an aberrant movement whose incubation and temporary triumph altered the trajectory of Western history, and Christianity and Islam have changed the character and histories of entire continents or sub-continents. Both were neither products of economic forces nor material conditions. They originated in the minds of fanatical and motivated schizophrenics who had the ability to convince masses of people to buy into their ideas, and individuals with the power to change the laws, rules, and customs of a society became members of these idealist creeds and decided to impose them on their societies, thus introducing them as causal factors in the unfolding of history. No impersonal forces to see here.

This, however, is not to say that there's no pattern to history. Rather, it is emphasizing the fact that linear history is a false theory. The past can be better than the present and the present can be better than the future. The Arab World during the Islamic Golden Age was a scientific capital of the world, but now it is nothing but a stain on the planet. It has had its Renaissance, but it is now intellectually degenerate, and without oil and the expertise of Western expatriates, no Arab nation would be economically and technologically advanced. Europe during the Middle Ages was inferior to the Hellinistic World in many respects, and it took until the Renaissance and the Age of Enlightenment to attain the same level of development again. History is like a wave. It is cyclical, not linear. It rises and falls. Ages of progress give way to ages of regression. The ascent of Empires opens the door to their descent. This pattern of crest and trough, high and low, is a proven constant of the human condition. It has been the lot of all human societies.

The United States seems to be going through its own age of decadence. It has peaked and is now declining. This should be

51

no shock or surprise to anyone who's familiar with the history of empires. Civilizations, after initial periods of vibrancy, eventually become bogged down in fatigue and inefficiency. They inevitably self-destruct. It has happened to every single one of them.

The question of how to make Golden Ages sustainable — how to make progress durable, how to make highs, ascents, crests, consistent and enduring — is the same the question of how to extend the natural lifespan of human beings, because nations and empires are born, they grow, they die, and permanently stay dead or become reborn. They follow the same pattern as organisms, because they're not driven by impersonal forces but by the appetites, characters and idiosyncrasies of the people that compose them.

In order to know how to stop people from aging and dying and make them immortal, it is necessary to know why people age and die. Similarly, in order to know how to bring about the meteoric rise of nations and avoid their degeneration and decline, it is important to know why nations and empires rise and fall. This is exactly what John Bagot Glubb tried to do in his book *The Fate of Empires and the Search for Survival*. He studied the major empires of history and noticed that they all followed the same pattern: (I) Pioneers (II) Conquest (III) Commerce (IV) Affluence (V) Intellect and (VI) Decadence, and this usually happened within a period of 250 years. America itself has followed exactly this pattern and is now trending towards decadence as it approaches its 250th year, which tallies well with Glubb's observations. This is why I consider Glubb worth reading for anyone who wants to understand why Empires rise and fall.

Other books to read for those who want to understand why Empires or nations experience fatigue are: *The Decline of the West* by Oswald Spengler, *The Study of History* by Arnold J. Toynbee (or you can read up on his Challenge and Response Theory for a brief overview), *Muqaddimah* by Ibn Khaldun, and *Why Civilizations Self-destruct* by Elmer Pendell.

If you want to read some interesting answers on how to avoid the fall and decline of nations and empires, you can read the following: *Imperium* by Francis Parker Yockey, *Revolt Against the Modern World* and *Ride the Tiger*, both by Julius Evola, and *The Fate of Empires: Being an Enquiry into the Stability of Civilizations* by Arthur J. Hubbard.

I don't necessarily agree with the authors, but I find them interesting. And the first two authors are especially exotic.

As for my own answer to the question, that would be a subject of an elaborately researched thesis in a future time.

If you're interested in having a better understanding of what's happening in the world on the geopolitical scale, you should read these two books at least: *The Clash of Civilizations* by Samuel P. Huntington and *The End of the World is Just Beginning: Mapping the Collapse of Globalisation* by Peter Zeihan.

Follow Tozara on Twitter: @TheSonOfMors

ON THE ANCIENT ORIGINS OF THE IRISH NATION AND THE POVERTY OF NATIONALIST MODERNISM

On the Ancient Origins of the Irish Nation and the Poverty of Nationalist Modernism

By Michael O'Donnell

The contention that nations and nationalism are a recent phenomenon has become cliché. Elie Kedourie defined nationalism by three propositions; humanity is naturally divided into nations, nations are known by certain characteristics, and the only legitimate government is national self-government.[1] For him, this idea was no older than the 19th century. Alongside Kedourie himself, the three most influential proponents of this view have been Ernst Geller, Eric Hobsbawm, and Benedict Anderson. Their theories vary in emphasis, yet they share a consensus that nationalism, imposed from above, created the nation and the emergence of nationalism was contingent on modernizing forces like centralized government, mass-media, standardized-education, and industrial-urbanism. Taking Ireland as its example, this essay contends that, nations and nationalism are pre-modern in origin, and many of the mechanisms for nationalist development which modernists associate strictly with modernization can be identified in premodernity.

Galli or "foreigners" is perhaps the single most used word in the medieval Irish Annals. The word appears as much as it does because from the 9th century onward, Norse Vikings persistently raided Ireland and established multiple ports. "Eodois, son of Donghal, suffered martyrdom from the foreigners at Disert-Diarmada… Maelciarain, son of Ronan, champion of the east of Ireland, a hero-plunderer of the foreigners, was slain," are typical entries, each from 867.[2] As the Viking era passed, *galli* was seamlessly transferred to Ireland's new Anglo-Norman invaders. While one word alone does not make a nation, it does evidence a certain consciousness. Social identity theory suggests that there is no way greater to sharpen an identity than to place it conflict. Minimal conditions, such as dividing people into groups A and B, are sufficient to produce in/out group behaviour.[3] This makes the constant use of 'foreigner' notable, as it presupposes an 'us' and a 'them'. In order for it to make sense, the reader must have an idea of who 'we' are. Its use could not simply have meant strangers from distant lands, either, because chroniclers insisted on using for centuries. Upon the arrival of Ireland's new Protestant invaders during the 16th-century Tudor conquests, the prevailing term for old Anglo-Norman invaders became *Seanghaill* ('Old Foreigners').

What shaped this shared consciousness before modernity? Beginning with beginnings themselves, nationalist discourse is often characterized as being preoccupied with origins. This was a well-developed discourse in Ireland, it having produced the largest body genealogical texts in medieval Europe.[4] The most influential of these is *Lebor Gabála Érenn*, meaning "The Book of the Taking of Ireland." [5] Complied in the early 11th century, though based on older poems, *LGE* outlines successive conquests of Ireland by six races, the most recent of which were the Milesian Gaels. The book is an attempt to contextualize Ireland's pre-Christian mythology within a grand narrative of Biblical history. In doing so, it imported an Israelite model of nationhood that tied together people, place, language, and religion. The Milesians are ultimately descended from Noah, through his son, Japheth, the forebear of all European nations. Coming to Ireland, the Milesians defeat the Tuatha Dé Danann, Ireland's pre-Christian gods, and the Fír Bolg, a malevolent race, and become Christian. As part of its biblically inspired narrative, the confusion of languages at the Tower of Babel is told, only with the addition that Fénius Farsaid, another descendent of Japhet who crafts Gaelic from the best fragments of the 72 languages that arose. Throughout the text, the forbearers of the other European nations appear, such as *Alba* (Scotland) and *Espa* (Spain). A world "naturally divided into nations" and "known by certain characteristics", is so integral to the one described in *LGE*, that it would be an understatement to say it evidences a nationalist worldview.[6] As a tale of such ambition, it would be more appt to call it nationalist cosmology.

Lebor Gabála Érenn would serve as the conventional account of Irish history well into the modern period. It was so widely believed that during the sectarian conflicts of early modernity, Irish exiles who fled to Spain were automatically granted the rights of Spanish subjects, on account of *LGE*'s claim that the Milesian Gaels had dwelt there before coming to Ireland.[7] Its contextualization of Irish myth within Biblical history poses several questions for the modernist hypothesis. Hobsbawm's tired cliché that premodern identity was either local or religious is undermined by the fact that it is the coming of Christianity which crystalizes the Gaelic nationhood in writing.[8]

For Gellner, the distinction between high and low culture is fundamental to his understanding of why nationalism cannot have been a pre-modern phenomenon. For him, nations are created by the "imposition of a high culture on society, where

previously low cultures had taken up the lives of the majority."
[9] This was only achieved in modern times because the elites of
pre-modern, politically decentralized societies, of which medieval Ireland is a prime example, had little interest in imposing
homogeneity. Far from taking no interest in low culture, *LGE* il-
lustrates literate ecclesiasts, educated in Christian and classical
literature, synthesizing Ireland's oral memory with biblical history. *LGE*'s valorization of the Irish language wouldn't sound
out of place among 19th-century Romantic nationalists, and certainly suggests its writer's consciousness extended beyond a
narrow preoccupation with particular aristocratic lineages. Its
vernacular Gaelic was already standardized island wide by the
9th century, due to the diligent work those same ecclesiasts.[10]
Thus the very process Gellner believes could only have occurred
in 19th century can be observed.

Benedict Anderson's argument is similar to Gellner's, but
focuses more on means. He argues that the infrastructure necessary for national identity was contingent on mass media, which
allowed for discursive communities of scale.[11] However, *LGE*
clearly attests to such an imagined community long before print.
It is true that few could read it, but its main form of transmission
would have been through Ireland's robust bardic tradition.
While discourse prior to mass communications would have been
less intensive, it also would have been less competitive. Sure,
there would have been no standardized curriculum, no man on
a screen to constantly remind you who your ancestors were and
where you came you from; but in the entire medieval and early
modern Gaelic literary canon, no one ever contradicts it either.
In the premodern cultural landscape, beliefs—particularly those
relayed by authorities like bards, bishops, priests, and kings—

would take hold among the non-literate and be reproduced indefinitely.

In making the case for medieval nations, we also need not limit ourselves to the airy matter of how pre-modern people understood themselves. Ireland's Brehon Law provides clear evidence of pre-modern cultural institutions with national scope. Codified in the 9th century, Brehon law was effectively a Gaelic school of jurisprudence. Well suited to the complex needs of Ireland's decentralized society, it was in use in Gaelic Ireland until the 17th century. Historian Neil McLeod notes that "Brehon law was 'national', in the sense that it was a cultural phenomenon of Ireland as a whole, with few (if indeed any) discernible regional variations." [12] Michael Richter similarly writes "Irish law knew of no boundaries of the *túatha*." [13] This lack of variation contradicts the notion that pre-modern culture was necessarily fragmentary, local, and unstandardized. In Brehon law we have a national institution, sustained over centuries, wholly apart from a centralized state, mass media, or any other such modernizing force. Modernization would of course bring immense changes, but in concluding that national customs simply couldn't be sustained before modernity, it is the modernists who are engaging in ahistorical projection of their own prejudices.

A common objection to the argument thus far is that it merely evidences ethnicity but not nationhood. '*Real*' nationalism mobilizes a public for political ends, modernists contend. Putting aside that the sharp distinction between nation and ethnicity is itself a product modernist prejudices, evidence of this can be gained by returning to the aforementioned trope of the foreigner in Irish literature. The subtly named *Cogad Gáedel re Gallaib*, meaning "The War of the Irish against the Foreigners" was produced by Brian Boru's great-grandson Muirchertach in

the early 12th century. It details Brian's wars against the Norse Uí
Ímair dynasty.[14] Intended to eulogize Brian and cement his dynasty, *CGrG* is highly propagandistic. The work was as effective
as it was (Brian is still widely regarded as one of the greatest
Irishmen to ever lived) because it was written in a tradition of
valorizing conflict between native and foreigner that by this
point was centuries old. As such, the authors spare no opportunity to valorize the Irish and demonize their enemies, though
in the spirit of the times, the Dane's are complemented for their
marital vigor:

> "Now on the one side of that battle were the shouting, hateful,
> powerful, wrestling, valiant, active, fierce-moving, dangerous,
> nimble, violent, furious, unscrupulous, untamable, inexorable,
> unsteady, cruel, barbarous, frightful, sharp, ready, huge, prepared, cunning, warlike, poisonous, murderous, hostile
> Danars; bold, hard-hearted Danmarkians, surly, piratical foreigners, blue-green, pagan; without reverence, without
> veneration, without honor, without mercy, for God or for man.
> But on the other side of that battle were brave, valiant champions; soldierly, active, nimble, bold, full of courage, quick, doing
> great deeds, pompous, beautiful, aggressive, hot, strong, swelling, bright, fresh, never weary, terrible, valiant, victorious
> heroes and chieftains, and champions, and brave soldiers, the
> men of high deeds, and honor, and renown of Erinn..."

Brian's Gaelic rival, Diarmaid mac Murchadha, the king
of Leinster, is cast as *"Demod of the Foreigners"*, *CGrG's* writers
being aware that it would reflect poorly on Diarmaid to emphasize his failure to side with his co-nationals. *CGrG* may not have
had the sustained reach of modern nationalist propaganda, but

it reflects similar underlying logic of national identity being mobilized in service of unity against a foreign threat.

Before his life was cut short at the Battle Clontarf (the battle described above) in 1014, Brian would proclaim himself *Imperator Scotorum*, Scoti being a synonym for Gael. His attempt to inaugurate a more centralized Gaelic national kingship would prove influential. Three centuries after Brian's death, the exiled Scottish king Robert de Bruce would evoke this idea to gain support from Irish chieftains, for whom the concept sill had resonance. De Bruce offered the chieftains an alliance against the English "so that our nation (*nostra natio*) may recover her ancient freedom." [15] He reminded the Irish that they and the Scots "stem from one seed of birth" and shared "a common language and common customs." While the configurations are different; today we would regard Ireland and Scotland as separate nations; the discourse is unmistakably nationalistic. De Bruce has even done us the convenience of giving us a precise definition of what he means by nation: "one seed of birth… a common language and common customs"; or, to put it more plainly, ancestry, language, and culture, each evoked to justify his claims and delegitimize the English. Domhnall O'Neill, one such chieftain persuaded by de Bruce's argument, wrote to the Pope in 1317 to elicit support for the effort. Referring to Scotland and Ireland as *Scotia Minor* and *Scotia Major* respectively, he charges that the English "have striven with all their might, and with every treacherous trick in their power, to wipe our nation out entirely." [16] If we are to take seriously the characterization of nations an 'imagined communities', then what possible grounds could we give for ignoring such a clear evocation of it?

One such argument, à la Gellner, is that the evidence presented thus far reflects only a tiny elite whose views were not necessarily shared by the wider population, and thus cannot be taken to evidence national consciousness. This is the case with all historical sources. They reflect the views of a person or group, and it is up to us to make informed assessments about what they say about the wider society. While this absence of evidence does give us cause to ask questions like 'what did the average medieval peasant actually know about Christianity?' it does not justify questioning whether Christianity even existed outside of monasteries. In order to sustain Hobsbawm and Gellner's sharp high/low distinction, we would have to believe that for centuries elites conducted nationalist discourses of the type evidenced in this essay—discourse used to rally armies, sing praises, and diminish rivals—but this discourse simply had no resonance beyond elites themselves. This is an unjustifiably solipsistic view of the pre-modern cultural landscape. Insofar as Brehon law "knew of no boundaries of the *túatha*", it already gives evidence that such boundaries were not as sharp as modernists like to think.[17]

Ireland ought to have presented a hard case for pre-modern nationalism, given how politically decentralized it was—yet two of Kedourie's criteria, a world divided into nations, which are known by certain characteristics, are unambiguously met before modernity. These assumptions are not only present in the medieval Irish worldview, but they are so integral to it that to try and make sense of them without understanding this would be as though you tried to understand them without knowing anything about their Christianity. Kedourie's third criterion, that the only legitimate government is national self-government, connotating as it does representative democracy in a centralized state, falls prey to the modernist prejudice of tautologically defining nations and nationalism by their 19th century instantiations. We don't define war by how it was practiced on Napoleonic battle-fields, so there is no reason to this for nations and nationalism. What we have seen that modernists are unjustified in trying to circumscribe mechanisms which act in service of national identi-ties, such as language standardization, nationwide institutions, and the shaping of the low by the high, wholly to modernity. Within the means of medieval technique, nationalistic discourses of ancestry, language, and culture were evoked to political ends such as inaugurating national kingship and expelling foreign rul-ers. These are one of many more appropriate applications for dealing with medieval nationalism's relation to governance and legitimacy. For these reasons, it is long overdue to admit that the modernist clichés that the people of the past had no powerful and enduring conceptions of themselves—every village its own nation—belongs as much to Tolkien as any of the romantic ex-cesses of the 19th century.

Endnotes

1. Kedourie, E. 1960. *Nationalism*. New York: Prager, p. 9.
2. 1856. *Annals of the Kingdom of Ireland*. Second Edition, Volume 1. Translated by J. O'Donovan. Dublin: Hodges, Smith, and Co.
3. Tajfel, H. & Turner, J. C., 1974. The Social Identity Theory of Intergroup Behaviour. *Social Science Information*, p. 65-93.
4. Ó Muraíle, 2005. P 193.
5. Toner, G., 2005. Lebor Gabála Érenn. In: S. Duffy, ed. *Medieval Ireland: An Encylopedia*. London: Routledge, p. 233.
6. Kedourie, 1960.
7. Walsh, M., 1979. The Military Order of St Patrick, 1593. *Seanchas Ardmacha*, 9(2), p. 280.
8. Hobsbawm, E. J., 1992. *Nations and Nationalism Since 1780*. 2nd ed. Cambridge University Press, p. 46-80.
9. Gellner, E., 1983. *Nations and Nationalism*. Ithaca: Cornell University, p. 57.
10. Richter, M., 2005. National Identity. In: S. Duffy, ed. *Medieval Ireland: An Encyclopaedia*. London: Routledge, p. 351-352.
11. Anderson, B., 1990. *Imagined Communities: Reflections on the Origins and Spread of Nationalism*. Revised Edition ed. London: Verso.
12. McLeod, N., 2005. Brehon Law. In: S. Duffy, ed. *Medieval Ireland: An Encyclopaedia*. London: Routledge, p. 42.
13. Richter, p. 351.
14. McLeod, p. 45.
15. Duffy, S., 2015. Crowning of Ireland's Last, Scottish High King.
16. Ibid.
17. Richter, p. 351.

Follow Michael on Twitter: @CyberHermetics

BLOWBACK:

INTELLIGENCE OPERATIONS IN THE
SOVIET-AFGHAN WAR, 1979-1989

Blowback:

Intelligence Operations During the Soviet-Afghan War, 1979-1989

By Galahad

"If we load up our leaders with this sort of analysis, their heads will explode"

This summation of the political situation of Afghanistan in 1978 by Aleksandr Orlov-Morozov, Deputy Station Chief of the KGB in Kabul, indicates the nation's complexity even before the invasion of the Red Army on Christmas Eve 1979.[1] For millennia, the area which is now Afghanistan has seen off attempts at its conquest. In 327 BC, Alexander the Great barely escaped the Kunar Valley with his life after having been struck by an arrow, and likely married Roxana in an attempt to pacify the Bactrian tribes occupying the Hidu Kush.[2] More recently Afghanistan played host to 'The Great Game', the contest between the British and Russian Empires for supremacy in the region. When the British found their position in Kabul untenable at the end of the first Anglo-Afghan War, they attempted to retreat in column to Jalalabad some 100 miles away with 16,500 soldiers and civilians. Over the course of a week from January 6 to

January 13 1842, the column was wiped out. Only one Briton, William Brydon, an assistant surgeon in the East India Company, made it to Jalalabad unmolested.[3] The British experience of Afghanistan inspired a verse in Rudyard Kipling's poem 'The Young British Soldier':

"When you're wounded and left on Afghanistan's plains, and the women come out to cut up what remains, jest roll to your rifle and blow out your brains an' go to your Gawd like a soldier"[4]

Afghanistan has more than earned its moniker: 'the Graveyard of Empires'.

It is perhaps little surprise then that, despite the overwhelming international condemnation of the Soviet invasion, it was predicted that few nations would go "further than their vote in the UN resolution."[5] According to analysis performed by the CIA, most nations saw Afghanistan as "a problem between the superpowers in which they should not become involved."[6] Of the nations that did involve themselves, a coalition of the United States, Pakistan, and Saudi Arabia took the lead. Their efforts formed the backbone of Operation Cyclone, the codename for the program through which the mujahadin—holy warriors fighting the Soviet Union in Afghanistan—would be armed and financed. This dissertation will examine the why these nations involved themselves in this covert action, what form their action took, how they contributed to the defeat of the Soviet Union, and the consequences of their actions in the years after the conflict.

"It should now be generally accepted that the Soviet Invasion of Afghanistan on Christmas Eve 1979 was deliberately provoked by the United States."[7] This is, at least, according to

Chalmers Johnson, one of the foremost authorities on the concept of 'blowback'. For him, blowback:

> "…does not just mean retaliation for the things our government has done to and in foreign countries. It refers to retaliation for the numerous illegal operations we have carried out abroad that were kept totally secret from the American public. This means that when the retaliation comes – as it did so spectacularly on September 11th, 2001 – the American Public is unable to put these events in context. So they tend to support acts intended to lash out against the perpetrators, thereby most commonly preparing the ground for yet another cycle of blowback." [8]

For a period of such importance, the Soviet-Afghan War is often overlooked. However, 9/11 spawned a renewed interest in Afghanistan and the role that Western powers (especially the US) have previously played in the region. As such, there is a broad literature on the US role in the conflict, much of which has been published in the last 20 years, and much of which has benefitted from the recent declassification of documents from the US Government.

Steve Coll, in his work *Ghost Wars*, provides a the most comprehensive account of the Soviet-Afghan War and its aftermath. His work is unique in so far as he has personally interviewed many of the most important actors in the Soviet-Afghan War, something which has been crucial to obtaining a more detailed representation of the conflict. Through the use of this privileged access, Coll's account provides a harsher critique of the actions of Pakistan and Saudi Arabia at the end of the Soviet-Afghan War and leadup to 9/11. His argument stands in contrast to the 9/11 Commission's Report, which Coll argues is "generous toward the Saudi government and the Pakistan Army", with the commissioners managing their criticisms of Riyadh and Islamabad "with future American counterterrorism partnerships in mind."[9]

Chalmers Johnson's 'Blowback series', comprising of *Blowback, The Sorrows of Empire, Nemesis,* and *Dismantling the Empire* is more assertive than Coll in his conclusion that the United States bears a large portion of the blame for not only the current state of the Middle East, but 9/11 itself. According to him, one can a trace a direct line between "the attacks on 11 September 2001 — the most significant instance of blowback in the history of the CIA — and the events of 1979."[10] His are more specific attacks against the actions of successive governments of the United States, rather than in depth studies of the Soviet-Afghan War.

As for a specific episode of the covert action, *Charlie Wilson's War* by George Crile offers an intimate examination of the 'Stinger Missile Crisis', and of one of the war's most enduring characters. Much like *Ghost Wars, Charlie Wilson's War* utilizes interviews and privileged access to sources to construct a detailed and engaging narrative which sheds light on the 'under-the-table' nature of the politics of covert action. Crile's account is immediately more favorable to the US, although he concedes that all significant events have "unintended consequences", and that it is undoubtedly the case that the Soviet-Afghan War "awakened the dormant dreams and visions of Islam."[11]

Due to the resurgence in interest in Afghanistan as a result of 9/11, there is a historiographical imbalance when it comes to the roles of Pakistan and Saudi Arabia in the conflict. As a result, secondary literature on the Pakistan and Saudi Arabian sections of this dissertation largely comes from academic essays. However, as the Soviet-Afghan War was one of Pakistan's most important foreign policy focuses since the nation's birth, there is copious debate regarding the costs and benefits of the Pakistani intervention.

This historiographical imbalance is also reflected in the choice of primary sources. Extracting primary material direct from the Pakistani and Saudi Arabian intelligence agencies (ISI and GID) was impossible, and neither government possesses declassified archives of any sort. As a result, this dissertation has relied extensively on the records of the Office of the Historian, the National Security Archive, and other declassified material direct from the CIA.

Chapter One

"We cannot afford to lose Afghanistan"

The following chapter will examine what motivated the Soviet Minister of Foreign Affairs Andrei Gromyko to make this statement in a meeting of the Soviet Presidium.[12] As such, the following will also seek to explain why the United States was so keen to deny Afghanistan to the Soviet Union.

The Soviet-Afghan War commenced amidst confusion. It has its beginnings in faulty intelligence and an inability to understand the religious, cultural, and political traditions and institutions in the region which came to plague both the US and the Soviet Union.

In the two decades leading up to 1978, the Soviet Union through the KGB had been supporting communists in leadership positions within Afghan universities and the Afghan Army. It is estimated that there were over 3,500 military personnel whose loyalties lay with the hammer and sickle, rather than the Afghan tricolor.[13] These Soviet aligned troops overthrew the Afghan President Mohammed Daoud in April 1978, and at the behest of their KGB handlers, launched a bloody campaign to eliminate all those who could threaten communist rule. By 1978 up to 12,000 political prisoners had been jailed, with religious and social leaders making up most of the numbers.[14] Many were executed.

The Soviet Union's fatal error in Afghanistan was its underestimation of the power of religion and tradition. Its secular reforms provoked even the most moderate Afghani Muslims. Directives from Moscow via Kabul outlawed dowries and Islamic lending systems, and implemented conscription, land seizures, and universal education, controversially including women. This socialist education and its exclusion of religion provoked the ire of a nation which had been dominated by Islam since the 9th Century.[15] A nation-state in name only, Soviet leaders who had learned their trade in a world of West vs. East, and capitalism vs. communism, could not comprehend the complexities of Afghanistan.[16]

These decrees could not have come at a more dangerous time. Inspired by the Iranian Revolution and Ayatollah Khomeini's rise to power, radical Shia activists began to cross the border into Afghanistan. The first signs of rebellion were found here, at the town of Herat on the Iranian Afghan border, in March 1979. A young army captain named Ismail Khan, outraged by ongoing religious persecution, led his garrison in a mutiny and began a jihad against the communist government. The future Governor of Herat Province, along with his troops, hacked to death dozens of communist advisors and their families, nearing a hundred in total.[17] As a result the Soviets sanctioned a response which would become a feature of their future campaign in Afghanistan. They razed Herat with vicious bombing runs, inflicting some 20,000 casualties.[18]

Searching for an explanation for the suddenness of the uprising, the Soviets were quick to look abroad. At a meeting of the Central Committee of the Soviet Union on March 17, 1979, Minister of Foreign Affairs Andrei Gromyko, argued that the insurgents in Herat had been trained and armed "not only with the participation of Pakistani forces, but also of China, the United States of America and Iran",[19] making them responsible for the atrocities in Herat. As regards US intervention, this is untrue. President Carter did not authorize the CIA to send money to the Mujahadin until July 3, 1979, at which point $500,000 was spent on propaganda, radio equipment, and medical supplies.[20] Eventually, the Politburo came to identify themselves and the communist regime and Kabul as part of the problem, stating in a June 28, 1979 report that "Taraki and Amin... none too rarely make mistakes and commit violations of legality", that "local bodies of revolutionary authority have not yet been created" and that the "recommendations of our advisors regarding these questions have not been put into practice."[21]

The situation soon deteriorated. In Kabul, Afghan President Nur Muhammed Taraki (who had bestowed upon himself the title 'Great Teacher') was overthrown in true Leninist style. The Communist Party had descended into factionalism, and a rival to the 'Great Teacher' had emerged in Hafizullah Amin. Although highly unpopular with the Politburo, Amin managed to overthrow Taraki, executing him on October 8, 1979. Although both had been directly funded by the KGB for years, Amin had steadily moved away from pursuing policy lines dictated by the Politburo as he gained power. He had at one point asked his Soviet advisor to withdraw Afghanistan's sovereign wealth fund (containing some $400 million) and place it into his personal account.[22]

After Amin's coup, the CIA detected a surge in activity along the Soviet-Afghan border. Reports detailed that the 105th Guards Airborne Division in the Turkestan Military District (now Uzbekistan) had been placed on full alert.[23] Although still skeptical of a full invasion, analysts correctly predicted that:

> "In expanding their own involvement in Afghanistan, there is a danger that the Soviets... will amplify their own stake in the ultimate outcome, making it increasingly difficult for them to

resist raising the level of their participation still another notch should they feel it necessary."[24]

By the end of 1979, the Soviet Union could no longer tolerate the situation in Afghanistan. Thanks to defectors from the Afghan Army, the Mujahadin numbered some 40,000, and were able to launch combat operations in 16 of the then 27 provinces of Afghanistan. The Amin regime only completely controlled the provinces of Kabul, Kunduz, and Baghlan.[25] On December 12, the CC CPSU agreed to "the execution of measures" ... in "A."[26] These 'measures' entailed a KGB assault on Tajbeg Palace (Amin's residence) in which Amin and his son were killed, the appointment of Babrak Karmal in his place, and the invasion of Afghanistan.[27]

There is a debate regarding the objectives and victory conditions of Operation Cyclone. In September 1979, just three months before the Soviet Invasion, a top-secret memo was sent by Thomas Thornton to President Jimmy Carter's National Security Advisor Zbigniew Brzezinski. Entitled "What Are the Soviets Doing in Afghanistan?", it was an amalgamation of all existing intelligence on the country. It began, "Simply, we don't know."[28]

Off the back of this, Steve Coll has argued that any suggestion of an American plan to lure the Soviets into Afghanistan and start a new Vietnam "warrants deep skepticism."[29] This assertion can be found in evidence, as Brzezinski cautioned President Carter that "the initial effects of the intervention are likely to be adverse for us", and that the US "should not be too sanguine about Afghanistan becoming a Soviet Vietnam."[30] However, Peter Dale Scott contends that Brzezinski, President

Carter's top cold warrior, "consistently exaggerated the Soviet menace beyond what saner heads at the time were estimating" and that "we should not believe what he wrote." [31]

Brzezinski's comments in 1998 offer some clarification. When asked if he had any regrets, Brzezinski replied: "Regret what? The secret operation was an excellent idea. It drew the Russians into the Afghan trap, and you want me to regret it?" [32] He further explained that although the US didn't make the Soviet Union intervene, by beginning their supply of the mujahadin in July 1979, they "knowingly increased the probability that it would." [33] If Brzezinski is to be believed, then the US succeeded in drawing the Soviet Union into the Afghan trap. The means and methods by which they would be kept there would range from the sublime to the ridiculous.

Chapter Two

The United States of America; Sting in the Tail

"Don't fuck it up, just go out there and kill Soviets, and take care of the Pakistanis and make them do whatever you need to make them do." [34] This is how the CIA Chief of Station in Islamabad Howard Hart understood his orders from Washington D.C. and was in effect the CIA strategy for the Soviet-Afghan War. An analysis of the US' role in the conflict is vital if one is to understand the final fall of the Soviet Union, and the rise of organizations such as the Taliban and Al-Qaeda. The way in which the US conducted their operations, and the sudden manner in which they washed their hands of Afghanistan left an unstable and crippled nation, out of which grew new threats to the west.[35]

Aid from the US to the mujahadin started off in rather modest fashion compared to the form that intervention would later take. According to the CIA, in the first six months of war (December 1979 to June 1980) the US had supplied some $30 million of equipment. This included some 4,000 AK-47s, 1200 Lee Enfield Rifles, 150 RPG-7s, and 7 million rounds of ammunition of various calibers, with double that amount expected in the next three months.[36] The method through which these weapons reached the mujahadin was complex. The arms originated in Egypt before being flown to Saudi Arabia. From there, the Saudis used their Hercules C-130 cargo aircraft to transport the munitions to Pakistan, where they were claimed by the ISI and smuggled over the Hindu Kush with the help of the mujahadin themselves.[37] This convoluted system was organized so that the US could still maintain a crucial "fig leaf of deniability." [38] In the early years of Operation Cyclone, the US was eager to avoid publicity, for fear of Soviet escalation and reprisals. It is for this reason that for the first years of the conflict, none of the weapons supplied to the mujahadin were sourced from US stock—almost all were from Eastern Bloc nations.[39]

Attempts to keep covert operations covert ended after 1980, when President Carter failed in his re-election bid, and Ronald Reagan acceded to the White House. With President Reagan came his doctrine, stating that the US would support "those who are risking their lives – on every continent from Afghanistan to Nicaragua – to defy Soviet aggression and secure rights which have been ours since birth." [40] This escalation led to arguably the most well publicized episode of the conflict, and one of the most infamous covert operations of all time. Immortalized in the film 'Charlie Wilson's War' (based on the book by George Crile), the mujahadin's acquisition of Stingers is seen by many as a turning point of the Soviet-Afghan War, and indeed of the whole Cold War, as it is likely that this is the first time American weapons were supplied with the specific purpose of killing Soviet troops.[41] In National Security Decision Directive 166 (a document that has never been fully declassified) President Reagan authorized the CIA to support the mujahadin "by all means available." [42] Along with Stingers, monetary support rose from $122 million in 1984, to $250 million in 1985, to $470 million in 1986, and $630 million in 1987.[43]

There is a debate over both the long term and short-term impact of Stinger missiles. Some were encouraged by reports of Stinger usage in Afghanistan. A heavily redacted report form the Commander of US Army Special Operations, stated that the impact of the Stinger has "favored the mujahadin, and altered the application of air power." [44] Furthermore, "more jets have been shot down with heavy machine guns since January 1987 than in any similar previous period",[45] owing to the fact that low level approaches from the Soviet Airforce were more common. These field reports tallied with concerns that the Soviets were relaying in talks between them, the US and Pakistan. In 1987, the Under-secretary of State for Political Affairs Michael Armacost relayed to Secretary of State George Schultz that the Soviet Ambassador to Afghanistan Yuli Voronstov "conceded that Soviet aircraft losses are up" and that he "registered concern with reports of additional Stinger deliveries."[46]

The reported effectiveness of the Stinger has led some to argue that its introduction into the conflict was the tipping point, after which Soviet failure was inevitable. Milton Bearden, CIA Station Chief in Pakistan by the end of the war, that the effect of the first Soviet helicopters being downed by Stinger missiles was "electric", and that within days, "the setbacks for Soviet forces were snowballing."[47] Likewise, Peter Rodman, President Reagan's Deputy National Security Advisor, has argued that "the escalation of US military aid to the Mujahadin, especially the furnishing of "Stinger anti-aircraft missiles"[48] played a crucial role in bringing the Soviet Union to the negotiating table. However, Alan Kuperman has been far more circumspect in his appraisal of the effect of Stinger missiles. He makes use of the fact that, unbeknownst to the US, Mikhail Gorbachev was attempting to remove the Soviet Union from Afghanistan the moment he came into office in March 1985, months before the first Stingers arrived in Afghanistan.[49]

Likewise, former high-ranking Soviets have maintained that US escalation did not provoke a Soviet withdrawal. Aleksandr Yakovlev, an advisor of Gorbachev, the Stinger "played no role. None"[50] in the cessation of hostilities. Former Soviet Foreign Minister Eduard Shevardnadze even argued that the Stinger "definitely prolonged our stay", as it "made our hawks more determined than ever not to withdraw, not to appear to be giving into duress." [51] From these reports, it seems to be that although the Stinger had an immediate military impact on the conflict, through the downing of helicopters and the forcing of the Soviets to change strategy, that it did not contribute to an early conclusion of the conflict, and might have in fact prolonged it.

This begs the question: what purpose did the weapons and money the US sent the mujahadin serve? An argument must be made that they provided the means with which a new generation of ideological enemies, this time Islamic fundamentalists, could begin their own global war. Terrorism was never on the radar of the US government, and there is little indication they had an understanding of the extremist forces they were unleashing. A memo, written in September 1980, details that the strength of tradition and Islam in Afghanistan and Pakistan dictates that any modern ideas, whether communist or Western, are seen as a threat,[52] but this is the extent to which the CIA worried about exactly who they were empowering. The US understood that religion was an important weapon against the Soviet Union, but they never believed it could one day be turned against them.

Ahmed Rashid sums up the fallout from Operation Cyclone thusly:

> "With the active encouragement of the CIA… some 35,000 Muslim radicals from 40 Islamic countries joined Afghanistan's fight. Tens of thousands more came to study in Pakistan's madrasahs. The camps in Pakistan and Afghanistan where they trained became virtual universities for promoting pan-Islamic radicalism. Americans only woke up to the danger in 1993, when Afghan-trained Arab militants blew up the World Trade

Center… the bombers believed that, just as Afghanistan had defeated one superpower—the Soviet Union—they would defeat a second." [53]

According to Charlie Wilson, who, perhaps more than anyone, influenced the decision to escalate Operation Cyclone, the US "fucked up the endgame." [54] It is a mistake to say there was one. By the time the Soviet Union withdrew its last armed forces on the 15th of February 1989, events were unfolding in Eastern Europe that beckoned the end of the Soviet Union, and thus distracted the US from Afghanistan. It returned to its pre-1979 policy towards Afghanistan, which comprised of "some humanitarian and economic aid" [55] but little in the way of policy focus. With up to a quarter of the Afghan population in refugee camps and the nation's infrastructure decimated by a decade of war, Afghanistan descended into an anarchy from which it is yet to truly recover. [56]

Chapter Three

Pakistan; "The Water Must Boil at the Right Temperature"

The above quote is from President of Pakistan Zia-ul-Haq, referencing the delicate balance of power within the mujahadin which needed to be maintained for Pakistani foreign policy goals to be met.[57] This chapter will examine the means and methods with which they, through the ISI (Inter-Services Intelligence bureau) attempted to control the outcome of the Soviet Afghan-War and analyze the consequences of their policies.

There is a consensus that without Pakistan, the mujahadin could not have defeated the Soviet Union. Marvin G. Weinbaum argues that without Pakistani involvement, "there could have been no effective Afghan resistance",[58] and Peter Dale Scott has labelled the ISI the gatekeepers of the Soviet-Afghan War.[59] President Zia, via the ISI, decided which mujahadin groups would receive the lion's share of supplies and training.

Pakistan was suffering from both internal and external instability. Since the Soviet invasion, Pakistan in effect shared a porous border with the Soviet Union, and since India still presented a threat from the east, Pakistan was under threat. As early as May 1978, Zia had warned Carter that "the advent of the leftist regime in Kabul is an event of historic proportions", and that India's close relationship with the Soviet Union meant that it would "act in tandem with it." [60] As such, Zia had two primary objectives. First, ensure the removal of Soviet forces from Afghanistan. Second, use the Afghan conflict to consolidate and solidify his regime at home by establishing a friendly, quasi-client state in Afghanistan and take advantage of Pakistan's role in the conflict to secure aid and concessions from the international community.[61]

The latter was the easiest to accomplish, as Zia took full advantage of his nation's status as lynchpin in Operation Cyclone. Aid commenced slowly in 1980, with "military sales resumed and facilitated", "the supply of 2 GEARING-class destroyers", and "additional assistance... to help deal with the Afghan refugee problem." [62] This aid program was later expanded to include $3.2 billion and permission to by F-16 fighter jets, despite warnings from the CIA that this technology would be shared with China, and despite the fact that Zia had been breaking his promises over Pakistan's nuclear program.[63][64] These concerns where shared by Carter who initially hesitated to send the fighter jets, but he was persuaded otherwise by Brzezinski, who argued that "the F-16 is all that we have to put in the pot with Zia." [65] Ultimately, the sale went through with the acknowledgement that the top secret technology in the F-16 would end up in unfriendly hands. Only after the close of the Soviet-Afghan War did this "wink-and-nod policy towards Pakistan's transfer of Washington's technology to Beijing" [66] come to an end.

Zia's domestic empowerment had several consequences for Pakistan. Although Zia was said to be "too much a politician to have the fundamentalist's fervor",[67] he built an internal alliance between "the military and the mullahs." [68] Zia had made no secret of plans to render inseparable Islam and the Pakistani State, once saying that since Pakistan was "created on the basis of Islam", that without it, "Pakistan would fail." [69] As he took official control of the Presidency in September 1978 (after having been Chief Martial Law Enforcer since July 1977), the US accepted that Zia would pursue a program of "Islamicization",[70] but hoped that it would act as a "legitimating force with which to build national unity." [71] This never came to fruition, as Zia used the mullahs to target secular political rivals. According to Irjaz Ahmad Khan, Zia's introduction of rigid interpretations of Islamic injunctions and jurisprudence contributed to a legacy that "continues to haunt the state and society of Pakistan",[72] thanks to "external assistance which secure(d) its very survival as a nation." [73]

Inextricably linked between the domestic bolstering of Islamism was the way in which Zia and the ISI chose to favor specific mujahadin groups in Afghanistan. The CIA had struggled to complete a full picture of the many factions of the mujahadin, admitting that their information on the insurgency was "uneven in quality and far from complete." [74] They could not compile "reliable information on which to base an estimate of insurgent strength"[75] due to the "possibly hundred"[76] insurgent groups in operation. The US also recognized that "without Zia's support, the Afghan resistance, key to making the Soviets pay a heavy price for their Afghan adventure, is [sic] effectively dead" [77] so they were happy to acquiesce to his demands to control arms and cash flow into Afghanistan. The mujahadin became "tools of Pakistan's Afghan policy",[78] giving Zia control over the political destiny of Afghanistan.

By 1982, Zia and the ISI had managed to merge some 80 separate mujahadin groups into seven Islamic and two secular parties, through a combination of bribery and politicking.[79] The seven Islamic factions (Hizb-e-Islami, Islamic Union for the Liberation of Afghanistan, Harakat Inqilab-e-Islam, Jamiat-e-Islami, National Islamic Front for the Liberation of Afghanistan, and National Liberation Front of Sibghatullah Mojaddedi) made up the Peshawar Alliance. The two secular parties, Afghan Millat and Shola-e-Javed, were ignored by Pakistan.[80] Zia had little time for non-religious, nationalist, and democratic forces, who had been considered a threat to Pakistan since its inception.

Over time, Hizb-e-Islami, led by Gulbuddin Hekmatyar, became the ISI's most favored party. From a Pakistani perspective, Hizb-e-Islami was a perfect tool with which to forge a new Afghanistan, amenable to Pakistani policy. Hekmatyar had been waging Jihad against one Afghani regime or another since the early 70s, much of which from exile in Pakistan, and his organization was considered to be "one of the best organized and most active" [81] in Afghanistan. Ideologically, in Hekmatyar, Zia had found an ally who shared his anti-communist zeal, and a leader who was already friendly with the Jamaat-I Islami Party of Pakistan, a close domestic ally.[82] This favoritism revealed itself most prominently in the allocation of US sourced weapons. Despite espousing increasingly vehement anti-US sentiment, it is estimated that of the millions of rounds of ammunition, thousands of rifles, and hundreds of mines and missiles,[83] Hizb-e-Islami received 20-25% of the total.[84] According to ISI Brigadier Mohammad Yousuf, who worked closely with Hekmatyar, the ISI felt as if they "could rely on him blindly." [85]

If the ISI was blind, the CIA was certainly in the dark. They underestimated both the size and importance of exile groups and had little understanding of their views. According to them, the exiled parties (of which Hizb-e-Islami was one) were "perhaps the least important of the insurgent groups." [86] Not only this, but the CIA had judged Hizb-e-Islami to be "more secular in outlook" than other groups.[87] Hekmatyar had been a committed fundamentalist for most of his adult life, having studied under Burhanuddin Rabbani and Abdul Rasul Sayyaff at Kabul University, two prominent Islamist scholars, both influenced by the Muslim Brotherhood and the works of Sayyid Qutb, one of the founders of Salafi jihadism.[88]

This goes to show the extent to which the US was blind to the problems it was creating, and the lengths to which Pakistan would go to promote its interests. William Pikeney, CIA Station Chief in Islamabad from 1984, was prophetic in his assessment of Hekmatyar and the Peshawar Alliance. Like many in Washington and Islamabad he admired Hekmatyar's ability as a warrior, but he felt uneasy whenever he met the mujahadin leader.

> "I would put my arms around Gulbuddin, and we'd hug, you know, like brothers in combat and stuff, and his coal black eyes would look back at you, and you just knew that there was only one thing holding this team together, and that was the Soviet Union." [89]

This is what came to pass. As soon as the Soviet threat passed, what little that united the Mujahadin disappeared, and, according to Shah Tarzi, the "fractured Afghan social structure reasserted its historical pattern by inducing and aggravating disunity and infighting among the muj." [90] Only now, the dozens of tribes and ethnic groups had hundreds of millions of dollars, advanced training, and advanced weaponry.

In the two civil wars that erupted after the Soviets left Afghanistan in 1989, Hekmatyar moved to systematically eliminate rival mujahadin groups, "serially kidnapping and murdering mujahadin royalists, intellectuals, rival party commanders—anyone who seriously threatened strong alternative leadership." [91] Hekmatyar turned his US and Pakistani supplied weapons onto the civilian population, and "pounded Kabul with rockets for three years" [92] (1992-1995), inflicting some 25,000 civilian casualties. Eventually, after the US led coalition's invasion of Afghanistan in 2001, Hekmatyar threw in his lot with the Taliban and the remnants of Al-Qaeda and encouraged Hizb-e-Islami mujahadin to fight against their former ally.

Zia never saw the end of the Soviet-Afghan War. He died in suspicious circumstances in a plane crash in August 1988, six months before the Soviet withdrawal. Nevertheless, the argument can be made that he achieved his immediate objectives. Soviet forces in Afghanistan were removed, domestic opposition was quashed, and the threat from an unfriendly Afghanistan dramatically diminished. However, these immediate successes gave way to profound problems.

Zia's alliance with extremists sparked a fundamentalist revival in Pakistan, which continues to contribute to immense sectarian violence. In the 1990s, some 2000 people were estimated to have been killed, and 561 injured in sectarian flashpoints in Punjab alone, the area with the highest number of madressahas (religious schools) in Pakistan.[93] The solidifying of Zia's rule allowed him to wield absolute power, and corruption in the arms pipeline meant that an estimated 50% of weaponry was stolen or sold, and some 30% of other covert aid went missing, turning Pakistan into one of the world's largest black markets for arms and ammunition.[94] Pakistan's leading role in the Soviet-Afghan came at a terrible cost.

Chapter Four

Saudi Arabia; Jihad for Sale

It was apparent to all nations involved that one of the most powerful weapons in the Soviet-Afghan War would be Islamic solidarity. Middle Eastern nations were only too happy to help counter what was seen as another atheist threat to a Muslim society. This chapter will focus on Saudi Arabian policy, the measures it took to support the mujahadin, and their consequences for Afghanistan and the world.

Within the current school of study of the Soviet-Afghan War, Egypt usually takes precedence when analyzing the effect that Arab nations had on the Soviet-Afghan War. This is understandable, as Egypt was among the first to commit to supporting the mujahadin, through weaponry and advisors, and maintained close ties to the US throughout the war.[95] Likewise, from Egypt emerged Islamists who would go on to form the core of the mujahadin, and some, like Ayman al-Zawahiri and Ahmad Shawqi-al Islambuli went on to be founder members of Al-Qaeda and other terrorist groups.[96] However, this has come at the expense of in-depth study of Saudi Arabia which, it must be argued, did more to promote violent fundamentalist Islam in Afghanistan and the broader Middle East than any other nation.

Saudi Arabia was eager to help the mujahadin, and equally eager to maintain their alliance with the US. Although judged to be reluctant to provide "any real support"[97] to the mujahadin in 1979 (Crown Prince Fahd had agreed not to send aid without General Zia's approval), by June 1980, perhaps sensing an opportunity to reaffirm Saudi Arabia's "privileged relationship" [98] with the US, Crown Prince Fahd had reportedly given his "unstinting support" [99] to Operation Cyclone. In a memo to President Carter, the Director of the CIA Stansfield Turner argued that this show of support would "impart new momentum" [100] to covert operations. Crown Prince Fahd's decision to match any and all US funding to the mujahadin was to prove of immense value.

Yet, Crown Prince Fahd and the Director General of Saudi Arabia's General Intelligence Directorate Prince Turki, were said to be "extremely sensitive" [101] to the nature of this covert action. They praised the "efficiency and security" [102] of the program but wanted to avoid having Saudi Arabia publicly linked with Operation Cyclone. In a meeting with Secretary of State Christopher Warren, Prince Saud claimed that this was in an attempt to avoid further acts of "Soviet imperialism and aggression", [103] given increasing levels of Soviet influence in North Yemen as a result of arms deals, which Crown Prince Fahd viewed as a direct threat to Saudi Arabia. However, there is another, more important reason as to why Saudi Arabia did not want a close association with Operation Cyclone.

Saudi Arabia was facing its own domestic problems. Since the late 1950s, Saudi Arabia had been inviting Egyptian radicals, usually Muslim Brotherhood academics from the prestigious al-Azhar University in Cairo, to teach in its own educational institutions. A rapidly modernizing nation, Saudi Arabia was undergoing an educational crisis, and saw the Muslim Brotherhood as a "source of qualified educators, bureaucrats and engineers", [104] all of whom were anxious to leave Egypt as a result of General Nasser's clampdown on the Brotherhood after his attempted assassination. By the late 1970s, many of the most important proponents of Islamist terrorism were educating in

Saudi Arabia, including Abdullah Azzam, Omar Abd al-Rahman, and Muhammad Qutb. It has been argued that Azzam, more than any other, laid the ideological foundations for Al-Qaeda, and is still considered "the strategic heart of Al-Qaeda." [105] Azzam was responsible for recruiting Osama bin-Laden, and sending him to Afghanistan for the first time.[106] Thus, thanks to Saudi education initiatives, a whole generation was exposed to fundamentalism through every level of education.

It is perhaps for this reason that Saudi citizens made up the largest group of foreign volunteers. It is alleged that the Saudi national airline even gave a "75% discount on airfare tickets to Pakistan to support travelers to Afghanistan who wished to answer the call of mobilization."[107] The Saudi royal family were more than happy to see them leave. Although official figures and research regarding terrorist attacks within Saudi Arabia are famously difficult to obtain given the still (relatively) closed nature of Saudi society, what is clear, is that there was a burgeoning class of religious extremists who were becoming increasingly displeased with the House of Saud's links to the West, and the perceived secularization of Saudi society.[108] This culminated in the seizure of the Grand Mosque at Mecca in 1979, by Sunni terrorists seeking the overthrow of the House of Saud. After a two-week siege, hundreds of militants, hostages, and security personnel were killed, with the Muslim world left in uproar. According to US Secretary of State Cyrus Vance, the 1979 'Mecca Incident' also stoked "Shia dissidence" [109] in the east of Saudi Arabia, and conspiracy theories regarding US involvement prompted Vance to re-examine the security situation of the "35 plus thousand Americans" in Saudi Arabia.[110] As such, fearing further instability, it is of little surprise Crown Prince Fahd and Prince Turki declared that they did not want to be publicly linked with the CIA in Afghanistan.

Following Osama Bin Laden and Abdullah Azzam out of Saudi Arabia were billions of dollars. Over the course of the war, Saudi Arabia spent $4 Billion per year on mosques, madrassas, preachers, students and textbooks to spread the Wahhabi creed over the next decades.[111] These camps and madrassas trained jihadis in Wahhabi ideology, and produced those militants who would form the Taliban and Al-Qaeda. In his work 'Knights Under the Prophets Banner', Ayman al-Zawahiri, one of the founders of Al-Qaeda, viewed the finance supplied by Saudi Arabia in Peshawar as indispensable. According to him:

> "A jihadist movement needs an arena that would act like an incubator, where its seeds would grow and where it can acquire practical experience in combat, politics and organizational matters." [112]

Peshawar and Afghanistan, awash with money and ideology, was that incubator.

It is noticeable that little of the fundamentalism and violence encouraged by the GID in Afghanistan made it back to Saudi Arabia. Thomas Hegghammer has noted that this seems "almost paradoxical", in light of the fact that "Saudi militants were so active abroad in the 1990s, either in guerrilla fighters in Afghanistan, Bosnia and Chechnya, or as members of… Al-Qaeda." [113] It has been argued that this may be a result of the result of Osama bin Laden's "strong relations with the Saudi intelligence and with our (Saudi Arabia) embassy in Pakistan." [114] According to Steve Coll, Bin Laden was said to have "a very good rapport with the ambassador and with all the Saudi ambassadors that served there" and there is some inference that this relationship continued until at least the late 1990s.[115] However, Hegghammer dismisses these ideas as "conspiracy theories" , stating that the lack of Al Qaeda operations in Saudi Arabia before 2003 can be explained by organizational factors.[116] He argues that before 1998, bin Laden "lacked the capability to mount the operations, while between 1999 and 2001 he lacked the intention",[117] and as a result, there was no need to espouse the theory that "the Saudi regime had literally paid off bin Laden in exchange for security." [118] Nevertheless, it is clear that 'the Land of the Two Holy Mosques' remained a critical source of money and fanatics for Al-Qaeda.

Whatever the relationship between the Saudi state and Al-Qaeda, success in the Soviet-Afghan War meant that Jihad was given new legitimacy. Carol and Jamsheed Choksy put it best in their work 'The Saudi Connection'. The Soviet-Afghan War:

> "…came to be seen as divine confirmation of jihad as necessary for Islam's global ascendance. Wahhabism in turn emerged as the 'indispensable ideology'… not just for the Saudi state but also for groups such as al-Qaeda, which took up the mission to enforce a purified form of Islam upon the world." [119]

Globalized Jihad rose from the same place the Soviet Union fell. The world moved into a new era.

Conclusion

"What is more important in world history? The Taliban or the Collapse of the Soviet Union? Some agitated Moslems or the liberation of Central Europe?"

The rhetorical question above, posed by Zbigniew Brzezinski in 1998, has lurked in the subtext throughout this examination of the Soviet-Afghan War and its consequences.[120] It is often used (as Brzezinski did) as a defense of the actions that the US and her allies took throughout the conflict, and as a way of redirecting responsibility for the current state of Afghanistan.

It is undoubtedly the case that the Soviet-Afghan War hastened the end of the Soviet Union. Whilst it is correct to caution that the Soviet Union was already in a state of decay by the 1980s, and that "economic dysfunction, political illegitimacy and institutional atrophy"[121] ran deeper than failed foreign intervention, in stating that, as Chalmers Johnson does, that "the demise of the Soviet Union owes more to Mikhail Gorbachev than to Afghanistan's partisans"[122] is to miss what prompted many of Gorbachev's reforms. There can be little debate that Afghanistan contributed to the end of the Brezhnev Doctrine, which mandated military intervention in nations where communism was under threat. In more practical terms, the years of military operations took an enormous toll on an already beleaguered economy, and "set in motion a round of East-West competition for which they were unprepared."[123] In this regard, the fact that by their own estimation, the CIA had consistently overestimated the strength of communist states since the late 1950s, and "failed to see the deterioration that led to the collapse of the communist regimes" led to the enormous scope of Operation Cyclone, and ensured that the Soviets failed in their Afghan adventure.[124]

As for the "agitated Moslems", it is important to remember that despite lurching from one tragedy to the next for the last 50 years, Afghanistan is not in a totally unique position as a political body.[125] Tom Lansford has argued that, like many other states still negotiating the legacy of colonialism, Afghanistan is "divided by ethnic and religious rivalries that reflect the legacy of the imperial powers and their acquisition and loss of territory." [126] Whilst this is undoubtedly true, it is only part of the story. Religious, ethnic, and tribal violence was the status quo long before 'The Great Game', that British effort to deny the subcontinent from the Russian Empire, was played. As Nasreen Akhtar states, "Afghanistan has never been a peaceful country", and "tribal rivalry and poverty" has not, does not, and never will, respect the rule of law.[127] As well, Afghanistan is politically and economically underdeveloped, and maintains its status as a rentier state, dependent on foreign aid for its survival. This was true before the Soviet invasion and had little to do with the actions of the US.

The problems Afghanistan faces today are the same as they have always faced. Like the British and Russian Empires before them, the Soviet Union, the United States, Pakistan, and Saudi Arabia did not create the religious, ethnic, and tribal strife which haunts 'the Graveyard of Empires'. Ironically, the United States, Pakistan, and Saudi Arabia created a unity in Afghanistan not seen for decades, if only for a short time, and if only motivated by the principle of 'the enemy of my enemy is my friend'. However, when that mutual enemy is defeated, the status quo always returns. In this case, like the British and Russian Empires before them, the Soviet Union, the United States, Pakistan, and

Saudi Arabia aggravated existing troubles, and symbolized by the infamous Osama bin Laden, created a new enemy.

The US' bullets and bombs, Pakistan's training and politicking, and Saudi Arabia's steady supply of cash and jihadis helped solve the problem of the Soviet Union, but sowed the seeds of a more mercurial and insidious opponent.

Operation Cyclone blew back.

Endnotes

1. National Security Archive, *Soviet Invasion a Case of Mission Creep,* October 13 2012, National Security Archive Electronic Briefing Book No.396.

2. Milton Bearden, *Afghanistan: Graveyard of Empires*, 'Foreign Affairs 80 (6)', (New York: Council on Foreign Relations, 2001).

3. William Dalyrmple, *Return of a King: The Battle for Afghanistan* (London: Bloomsbury Paperbacks, 2014), p. 387.

4. Rudyard Kipling, *The Young British Soldier.*

5. Central Intelligence Agency, National Foreign Assessment Council, *Worldwide Reaction to the Soviet Invasion of Afghanistan: An Intelligence Memorandum,* 1980, p. ii.

6. Ibid, p. i.

7. Chalmers Johnson, *Abolish the CIA!*, 'London Review of Books 26 (20)', (London: London Review of Books, 2004).

8. Chalmers Johnson, *Nemesis: The Last Days of the American Republic* (New York: Metropolitan Books, 2008), p. 278.

9. Steve Coll, *Ghost Wars: The Secret History of the CIA, Afghanistan, and Bin Laden, From the Soviet Invasion to September 10 2001* (London: Penguin Books, 2004), p. 588.

10. Chalmers Johnson, *Abolish the CIA!*

11. George Crile, *Charlie Wilson's War* (London: Atlantic Books, 2007), p. 520.

12. David C. Gompert, Hans Binnendijk and Bonny Lin, *Blinders, Blunders and Wars: What America and China can Learn* (Santa Monica: RAND Corporation, 2014), p. 129.

13. Larry P Goodwinson, *Afghanistan's Endless War: State Failure, Regional Politics, and The Rise of The Taliban.* (Seattle: University of Washington Press, 2015), p. 51.

14. Sir Martin Ewans, *Afghanistan.* (London: Routledge, 2015), p. 142.

15. David C. Gompert, Hans Binnendijk & Bonny Lin, *Blinders Blunders and Wars: What America and China Can Learn* (RAND Corporation, 2014), p. 130.

16. Ibid, p. 131.

17. Steve Coll, *Ghost Wars.* (New York, N.Y: Penguin Books, 2005), p. 41.

18. Ibid.

19. Woodrow Wilson Centre, *Transcript of CPSU CC Politburo Discussions on Afghanistan,* March 17 1989, History and Public Policy Program Digital Archive, p. 2.

20. Coll, p. 46.

21. Woodrow Wilson Centre, *Report on the Situation in Afghanistan, Gromyko, Andropov, Ustinov and Ponomarev to CPSU CC,* History and Public Policy Program Digital Archive, p. 2.

22. Vasily Mitrokhin, *The KGB in Afghanistan.* (Washington D.C: Woodrow Wilson International Centre for Scholars, 2002), p. 46.

23. CIA, *The Soviet Invasion of Afghanistan: Implications for Warning,* September 1980, p. 26.

24. Ibid.

25. Aleksandr Antonovich Lyakhovsky, *Inside the Soviet Invasion of Afghanistan and the Seizure of Kabul, December 1979* (Washington D.C.: Woodrow Wilson Center, 2007), p. 3.

26. National Security Archive, *Concerning the Situation in 'A',* Resolution of the CC CPSU, December 12 1979, p. 2.

27. Lyakhovsky, p. 50.

28. The National Security Archive, *What Are The Soviets Doing In Afghanistan?,* 1979, p. 1.

29. Coll, p. 593.

30. The National Security Archive, *Reflections on the Soviet Invasion in Afghanistan,* 1979

31. Peter Dale Scott, *The Road to 9/11: Wealth, Empire, and the Future of America* (Berkley: University of California Press), p. 254.

32. Vincent Jauvert, *Les Revelations d'un ancient conseiller de Carter,* Le Nouvel Observateur (Paris: Groupe Nouvel Observateur, 1998), p. 76.

33. Ibid.
34. Howard Hart interviewed by Steve Coll (November 26th and November 27th, 2001) in Steve Coll, *Ghost Wars*, p. 55.
35. George Crille, *Charlie Wilson's War* (London: Atlantic Books, 2007).
36. Office of the Historian, *Memorandum Prepared in the Central Intelligence Agency*, June 11 1980, Foreign Relations of the United States, 1977-1980, Volume XII, Afghanistan.
37. Ibid.
38. Charles G. Cogan, *Partners in Time: The CIA and Afghanistan since 1979*, 'World Policy Journal 10(2)', (Durham: Duke University Press, 1993), p. 76.
39. Ibid.
40. Chester Pach, *The Reagan Doctrine: Principle, Pragmatism, and Policy*, 'Presidential Studies Quarterly 36 (1)', (Washington D.C.: The Center for the Study of the Presidency, 2006), p. 76.
41. Alan J. Kuperman, *The Stinger Missile and US Intervention in Afghanistan*, 'Political Science Quarterly 114 (2)', (New York: Academy of Political Science, 1999), p. 219.
42. Ibid, p. 227.
43. Oliver Roy, *The Lessons of the Soviet/Afghan War* (London: Brassey's, 1991), p. 35.
44. National Security Archive, *Commander, US Army Operations Group, Impact of the Stinger Missile on Soviet and Resistance Tactics in AF*, 1987, National Security Archive Electronic Briefing Book No. 34.
45. Ibid.
46. Office of the Historian, *Memorandum from the Under Secretary of State for Political Affairs (Armacost) to Secretary of State Schultz*, March 20 1987, Foreign Relations of the United States, 1981-1988, Volume VI, Soviet Union, October 1986-January 1989.
47. Milton Bearden, *Afghanistan: Graveyard of Empires*, 'Foreign Affairs 80 (6)', (New York: Council on Foreign Relations, 2001), p. 22.
48. Peter Rodman, *More Precious than Peace: Fighting and Winning the Cold War in the Third World* (New York: Scribner, 1994), p. 221.
49. Kuperman, *The Stinger Missile*, p. 236.
50. Charles G. Cogan, *Partners in Time: The CIA and Afghanistan since 1979*, 'World Policy Journal 10(2)', (Durham: Duke University Press, 1993), p. 74.
51. Kuperman, *The Stinger Missile*, p. 236.
52. National Security Archive, *Central Intelligence Agency, Directorate of Intelligence, Office of Political Analysis, The Soviets and the Tribes of Southwest Asia*, September 23 1980, National Security Archive September 11th Sourcebook Volume II.
53. Ahmed Rashid, *The Taliban: Exporting Extremism*, 'Foreign Affairs 78 (6)', (New York, Council on Foreign Relations, 1999), p. 32.
54. Crille, *Charlie Wilson's War*, p. 252.
55. Tom Lansford, *A Bitter Harvest: US Foreign Policy and Afghanistan* (Aldershot: Ashgate, 2003), p. 129.
56. Andrew Hartman, *'The Red Template': US Policy in Soviet-Occupied Afghanistan*, 'Third World Quarterly 23 (30)', (Oxford: Routledge, 2002), p. 483.
57. Steve Coll, *Ghost Wars* (London: Penguin Books, 2004), p. 63.
58. Marvin G. Weinbaum, *War and Peace in Afghanistan: The Pakistani Role*, Middle East Journal 45 (1), (Washington D.C.: Middle East Institute, 1991), p. 71.
59. Scott, *The Road to 9/11*, p. 125.
60. Office of the Historian, *Letter from Pakistani General Zia to President Carter*, May 9 1978, Foreign Relations of the United States, 1977-1980, Volume XII, Afghanistan.
61. Weinbaum, *War and Peace in Afghanistan*, p. 73.
62. The Office of the Historian, *Memorandum from the President's Assistant for National Security Affairs (Brzezinski) to Secretary of State Vance*, January 2 1980, Foreign Relations of the United States, 1977-1980, Volume XIX, South Asia.

63. Dennis Kux, *The United States and Pakistan 1947-2000: Disenchanted Allies* (Washington D.C.: Woodrow Wilson Centre Press) p. 256-257.

64. The National Security Archive, *George Shultz to Ronald Reagan: How Do We Make Use of the Zia Visit to Protect Our Strategic Interests in the Face of Pakistan's Nuclear Weapons Activities?*, November 26, 1982.

65. Office of the Historian, *Memorandum from the President's Assistant for National Security Affairs (Brzezinski) to President Carter*, October 1 1980, Foreign Relations of the United States, 1977-1980, Volume XIX, South Asia.

66. Jonah Blank, *Pakistan and China's Almost Alliance* (Santa Monica: RAND Corporation)

67. Muhammad Yousuf, *Silent Soldier: The Man Behind the Afghan Jihad* (Lahore, Jing Publishers, 1991), p. 99.

68. Ijaz Ahmad Khan, *Understanding Pakistan's Pro-Taliban Policy*, Pakistan Horizon 60 (2), (Karachi: Pakistan Institute of International Affairs, 2007), p. 145.

69. Mary Ann Weaver, *Pakistan: Deep Inside the World's Most Frightening State* (New York: Farrar, Straus and Giroux), p. 61.

70. Office of the Historian, *Telegram from the Embassy in Pakistan to the Department of State*, September 15 1978, Foreign Relations of the United States, 1977-1980, Volume XIX, South Asia.

71. Ibid.

72. Khan, 2007, p. 145.

73. Ibid.

74. Office of the Historian, *Memorandum Prepared in the Central Intelligence Agency*, August 8 1980, Foreign Relations of the United States, 1977-1980, Volume XII, Afghanistan.

75. Ibid.

76. Ibid.

77. National Security Archive, *George Schultz to Ronald Reagan: How Do We Make Use of the Zia Visit to Protect Our Strategic Interests in the Face of Pakistan's Nuclear Weapons Activities?*, November 26 1982,

National Security Archive Electronic Briefing Book No. 377.

78. Khan, 2007, p. 151.

79. Weinbaum, 1991, p. 151.

80. Mohammad Yousuf and Mark Adkin, *The Bear Trap: Afghanistan's Untold Story* (London: Leo Cooper, 1991) p. 40.

81. *Memorandum Prepared in the Central Intelligence Agency*, August 8 1980.

82. Weinbaum, p. 77.

83. Office of the Historian, *Memorandum from Director of Central Intelligence Turner to the President's Assistant for National Security Affairs (Brzezinski)*, March 6 1980, Foreign Relations of the United States, 1977-1980, Volume XII, Afghanistan.

84. Weinbaum, p. 78.

85. Barnett R. Rubin, *The Fragmentation of Afghanistan: State Formation and Collapse in the International System* (New Haven, Yale University Press, 2002), p. 232.

86. Office of the Historian, *Memorandum Prepared in the Central Intelligence Agency*, August 8 1980, Foreign Relations of the United States, 1977-1980, Volume XII, Afghanistan.

87. Office of the Historian, *Memorandum Prepared in the Central Intelligence Agency*, January 9 1980, Foreign Relations of the United States, 1977-1980, Volume XII, Afghanistan.

88. Coll, 2004, p. 113.

89. Steve Coll, *Interview with William Piekney*, January 14 2002, in *Ghost Wars*, p. 120.

90. Shah M. Tarzi, *Politics of the Afghan Resistance Movement: Cleavages, Disunity, and Fragmentation*, 'Asian Survey 31 (6)', (California: University of California Press, 1991), p. 484.

91. Open Society Foundations, *Casting Shadows, War Crimes and Crimes Against Humanity 1978-2001*, 'The Afghanistan Justice Project' (London: Open Society Foundations, 2005), p. 59.

92. Ibid, p. 63.

93. A.Z. Hilali, *The Costs and Benefits of the Afghan War for Pakistan*, 'Contemporary

South Asia 11 (3)' (London: Taylor and Francis, 2002), p. 304.

94. Jan Goodwin, *Caught in the Crossfire* (London: Sphere Publishing), p. 45-46.

95. Pervez Hoodbhoy, *Afghanistan and the Genesis of Global Jihad*, 'Peace Research 37(1)', (Winnipeg: Canadian Mennonite University, 2005), p. 2.

96. Ibid.

97. Office of the Historian, *Intelligence Information Cable Prepared in the Central Intelligence Agency*, March 27 1979, Foreign Relations of the United States, 1977-1980, Volume XII, Afghanistan.

98. Office of the Historian, *Memorandum from the President's Assistant for National Security Affairs (Brzezinski) to Secretary of State Vance and Secretary of Defense Brown*, March 14 1980, foreign Relations of the United States, 1977-1980, Volume XVIII, Middle East Region; Arabian Peninsula.

99. Office of the Historian, *Memorandum From Director of Central Intelligence Turner to President Carter*, July 7 1980, Foreign Relations of the United States 1977-1980, Volume XIII, Afghanistan.

100. Ibid.

101. Office of the Historian, *Memorandum Prepared in the Central Intelligence Agency*, June 11 1980, Foreign Relations of the United States 1977-1980, Volume XII, Afghanistan.

102. Ibid.

103. Office of the Historian, *Telegram from the United States Liaison Office in Riyadh to the White House*, February 5 1980, Foreign Relations of the United States, 1977-1980, Volume XVIII, Middle East Region; Arabian Peninsula.

104. Trevor Stanley, *Understanding the Origins of Wahhabism and Salafism*, 'Terrorism Monitor 3 (14)', (Washington D.C.: The Jamestown Foundation, 2005).

105. Yousuf Aboul-Enein, *The Late Sheik Abdullah Azzam's Books: Part 2: Remedy for Muslim Victimisation* (New York: Combatting Terrorism Centre at West Point, 2008), p. 3.

106. Ibid.

107. Muhammad Haniff Hassan, *Mobilisation of Muslims for Jihad: Insights from the Past and their Relevance Today*, 'Counter Terrorist Trends and Analyses 5 (8)' (Singapore: International Centre for Political Violence and Terrorism Research, 2013), p. 12.

108. Thomas Hegghammer, *Jihad, Yes, But Not Revolution: Explaining the Extraversion of Islamist Violence in Saudi Arabia*, 'British Journal of Middle Eastern Studies 36 (3)' (Oxford: Taylor & Francis Ltd., 2009), p. 400.

109. Office of the Historian, *Memorandum from Secretary of State Vance to President Carter*, November 28 1979, Foreign Relations of the United States, 1977-1980, Volume XVIII, Middle East Region; Arabian Peninsula.

110. Ibid.

111. Carol E.B. Choksy and Jamsheed K. Choksy, *The Saudi Connection: Wahhabism and Global Jihad*, 'World Affairs 178 (1)' (Washington D.C.: Sage Publications Inc., 2015), p. 27.

112. Ayman al-Zawahiri, *Knights Under the Prophet's Banner*, in Steve Coll, *Ghost Wars*, p. 154.

113. Thomas Hegghammer, *Islamist Violence and Regime Stability in Saudi Arabia*, 'International Affairs 84(4)', (Oxford: Oxford University Press, 2008), p. 701.

114. Coll, *Ghost Wars*, p. 88.

115. Ibid.

116. Hegghammer, *Jihad, Yes But Not Revolution*, p. 415.

117. Thomas Hegghammer, *Islamist Violence and Regime Stability in Saudi Arabia*, 'International Affairs 84(4)', (Oxford: Oxford University Press, 2008), p. 709.

118. Ibid.

119. Choksy and Choksy, *The Saudi Connection*, p. 27.

120. Vincent Jauvert, *Les Revelations d'un ancient conseiller de Carter*, Le Nouvel Observateur (Paris: Groupe Nouvel Observateur, 1998), p. 76.

121. David C. Gompert, Hans Binnendijk and Bonny Lin, *Blinders, Blunders and Wars: What America and China can Learn* (Santa Monica: RAND Corporation, 2014), p. 130.

122. Chalmers Johnson, *Abolish the CIA!*, 'London Review of Books 26 (20)', (London: London Review of Books, 2004).

123. Gompert et al., *Blinders, Blunders and Wars*, p. 130.

124. Douglas J. MacEachin, *CIA Assessments of the Soviet Union: The Record Versus the Charges*, (Langley: CIA), p. 8.

125. Jauvert, 1998, p. 76.

126. Lansford, *A Bitter Harvest: US Foreign Policy and Afghanistan*, p. 184.

127. Nasreen Akhtar, *Pakistan, Afghanistan and the Taliban*, 'International Journal of World Peace 25 (4)', (Minnesota: Paragon House, 2008), p. 50

About the Author:

Galahad is an aspiring corrupt public official.

Follow him on Twitter: @_galaaus

AN EMPIRE OF MAGICK:

OCCULTISM
& THE BRITISH EMPIRE

An Empire of Magick: Occultism & the British Empire

By Justin Geoffrey

In the popular mind, occultism is synonymous with diabolism. Thanks to decades of horror films, as well as the popularity of paranormal television programs like *Ghost Hunters* or *Paranormal Adventures,* the occult conjures forth ideas about black magick, demonic possession, and legions of other infernal activities. Those who dabble in the occult are deemed either wicked or ignorant of the ramifications. Most importantly, popular culture tends to see occultism as the purview of individuals, or the plaything of small, highly secretive cults.

However, since 2016, the rise in popularity of Q-Anon, an Internet-based theory that broadly sees Satanic and pedophilic elites as the core engine driving economic globalism and social progressivism, has rekindled interest in another theme of occultism — the role of occultism and occult practices in the exercise of state power. While adherents to Q-Anon are wantonly cast aside as cranks and "conspiracy theorists", a scholar such as Ioan Couliano cannot be. In his work *Eros and Magic in the Renaissance,* Couliano argues that the Renaissance and the Early Modern Period formed the "magician State." A subtle and flexible state with the "capacity to change, to adapt to all circumstances, to improve", Couliano positively identifies the magician State as preferable to its supposed opposite, the police State.[1] Couliano's magician State is one built upon eros, which he claims "represents the starting point of all magic."[2] Erotic images and ideas are cultivated by the magician State in order to secure its power via widespread acceptance of the desirability of state-cultivated eroticism. The clearest example of this in practice comes from the world of advertising. Advertisers use the "magic" inherent in media and images to sell their products to the mass of consumers. Often, the magic that proves the most effective is emotional, with eroticism traditionally predominating (although "sex sells" does not appear as prevalent as it was in the late 1990s and early 2000s).

The magician State, which began when Europe's many rulers, especially those in Northern Italy, brought into their courts alchemists and sorcerers, rules by thought control. A magician State uses its power of manipulation to *convince* its subjects that they are free, or that they are living in the preferred state of socio-political being. When these opinions or desires change, the magician State uses its subtle power to misdirect or redirect these energies back towards those states of being that do not challenge the magician State. For Couliano, the magician State's primary weakness is the ever-present possibility of devolving into what he terms the sorcerer-State, wherein the magicians in control of the state become too enamored with their own power.[3] Tellingly, the police State is the opposite of the magician State but does not ultimately threaten it. Rather, according to one of Couliano's students, writer and magician John Michael Greer, the magician State is most threatened by chaos magick in the form of antediluvian democracy.[4] The cybernetic and often real war between the magician State and chaos magick has characterized much of American socio-political life since 2016, with the supporters of President Donald Trump and adjacent right-wing movements (including Q-Anon) cast in the role of chaos agents seeking to thoroughly undermine America's magician State.

The relationship between magic, occultism, and the state may be older than recorded history. Hunter-gatherer tribes had secret societies complete with ritual associations and esoteric knowledge that members guarded with extreme violence.[5] These primordial cults often had a biological character, with the social elite, whether heroic or deformed, originating in these highly occult bodies. As such, it can be stated with pervasive evidence that occult practices are integral to state formation and state power, and always have been. The difference between states, therefore, is a matter of magic.

In the 20th century, no state better exemplified black magic than the Third Reich. Historian Nicholas Goodrick-Clarke, who was one of the first scholars to seriously study the occult roots and practices of German National Socialism, characterized the Third Reich as "the embodiment of evil…a monstrous pagan relapse in the Christian community of Europe." [6] The Third Reich's quest for German *lebensraum*, as well as its many investigations into Theosophy, pagan rites, etc., continue to mark it is as an abhorrent state that made magick both integral and visible. Other states, most notably in Africa and the Caribbean, had similar state occultism. Most of them were characterized by strongman dictators who used religion (François Duvalier in Haiti) or their own eccentric ideas (Eric Gairy with UFOs in Grenada) and secret police forces to control the public and private lives of their citizens. Others, such as Idi Amin in Uganda, resorted to the vilest practices of black magick such as cannibalism in order to maintain their power. Such brutal and unsubtle magician States contribute to sensationalism while also obscuring other states which used magick and occultism to pursue their own geopolitical goals. Chief among these states was the Kingdom of England during its first age of imperialism.

Under the reign of Queen Elizabeth I (1558-1603) and King James I (1603-1625), the Kingdom of England saw its status as a naval power increase thanks not only to its thwarting of a planned Spanish invasion, but also its creation of colonies (called "plantations") in Ireland and the New World. Many of these imperial ventures were undertaken by private individuals using their own ships ("privateers"). Many of these men had interests in alchemy. For instance, Sir Walter Raleigh used his many travels in the New World to not only search for the fabled golden city of El Dorado, but he also took samples of American flora and fauna back to England to be used in his many alchemical experiments. The other great seafarer of the age, Sir Francis Drake, codenamed *Water* by the Virgin Queen, was rumored to have occult powers. The rumor proved so strong that both English and Spanish prisoners told stories about the admiral's prowess.[7] Indeed, the entirety of the original English goals in the New World conformed to an esoteric premise, i.e. the creation of a new civilization. The English expeditions under Raleigh and others frequently allied with colonies of escaped slaves, both African and Mesoamerican, in Central America in order to plunder the Spanish treasure ships. Serious plans were afoot too that would have seen these former captives brought to English colonies in North America as free settlers.[8]

John Dee – Scholar, Spy, and Summoner of Angels

But in regards to occultism and the English Empire (later to become the globe-spanning British Empire), no figure is more important than John Dee. Dee (1527-1608) was a natural philosopher, mathematician, and occultist. He was also the private and highly secretive intelligence agent for Queen Elizabeth I's court. He began his studies at St. John's College, Cambridge in 1542, where he earned a bachelor's degree and a graduate degree. From there, Dee was named a fellow at Trinity College, Cambridge upon its founding in 1546. Between 1547 and 1551, Dee traveled throughout Europe, with special attention paid to the Low Countries. Dee studied under many notable alchemists and philosophers, including the Flemish cartographers Abraham Ortelius and Gerardus Mercator, as well as other well-known mathematicians.

Following his return to England, Dee became a professor of mathematics at Oxford. It was his knowledge of mathematicians and cartography that earned him entrance into the royal court as a teacher. Dee specialized in instructing mathematics to naval captains, the chief conquerors of the English people. Dee's proficiency in mathematics and science (he was an early proponent of heliocentrism) earned him the ear of Queen Elizabeth. The scholar was tapped as a resource in the war between England and Spain.

In the late 16th century, the enormity of Spain's power could not be fully measured. The Catholic kingdom controlled not only one of the richest empires in Europe, which included the Low Countries and hereditary states in Italy, but also commanded the vast resources of Mexico, Peru, and the Caribbean. Spanish treasure ships regularly crossed the Atlantic with fabulous hordes of gold and silver. Only England, the chief Protestant power in Europe, could disrupt Spanish imperium. For the most part, these disruptions amounted to privateering raids on Spanish possessions and robberies on the high seas. By 1588, Spain decided to destroy England and her navy once and for all. In May of that year, Spanish King Philip II sent 125 of his best ships to the English Channel. His goal was to destroy English ships and claim the Channel as a Spanish protectorate. Awaiting him were the best English sailors of the age, and John Dee.

Eight years previously, Dee had spent time in Central Europe as the guest of the Polish nobleman Count Adalbert Laski. Dee eventually found his way to Prague, a city then reputed to be the epicenter of Catholic intrigues against Protestants.[9] Given Dee's later position as the chief spymaster for Queen Elizabeth, it is possible that the court magician used his time in Prague to learn more about Spanish machinations against England. Whatever the case, it was Dee who made the fateful decision to advise the Queen to keep her ships at bay. While many among the Spanish believed that the English wizard had conjured up the dreadful storm himself, it is more likely that Dee utilized his knowledge of meteorology to accurately predict the tremendous storm that doomed the Spanish Armada.

Throughout his years of loyal service to Queen Elizabeth, Dee consistently proved himself to be an exponent of English expansionism. The court magician sought this ideal in multi-faceted ways. For one, as previously noted, Dee became one of England's first spymasters—an intelligence agent who used his wide learning and many connections to discover the secrets of England's adversaries. Few of Dee's exploits are known. For instance, while touring the University of Louvain in Belgium, Dee purloined cutting-edge astronomical instruments and two globes that were then the most accurate in the world.[10] Such items would be put to good use by the Royal Navy or by English privateers. Dee's other exploits on the Continent are not as well known to history, but one can be sure that the magician did many deeds, possibly even nefarious ones, in order to increase the power and prestige of the English crown. Of note is the fact that Dee designed his own secret cipher for all his communications back to London. "For your eyes only" was his designation for all communications to Queen Elizabeth, while the alchemist used the magically important number seven and two eyes to create his unique signature—007.[11] Thus, long before Ian Fleming—himself an officer in naval intelligence during World War II—created James Bond, John Dee played the role of England's chief spy and charmer.

Dee's espionage and government work cannot and should not be decoupled with his other interests. Occult practices formed the core mission of Dee's work, from underhanded diplomacy to his attempts to communicate with angels. In his last years, Dee became obsessed with the possibility of directly communicating with celestial beings. For thirty years, Dee used his knowledge of optics (including the reported use of a magical Aztec obsidian mirror) and scrying (the act of looking into polished stones like crystal balls in order to tell the future) to discover and document the so-called Enochian language of the angels. This era of Dee's life included a rather shady character by the name of Edward Kelley, a twentysomething alcoholic with deformed ears thanks to a previous conviction for counterfeiting coins.[12] Together, Dee and Kelley kept so-called "spirit diaries" that detailed their communications with spirits. These experiments lasted for ten years or more. During that time, Dee gave the Enochian language its own grammar and syntax, thus making it a fully formed, albeit artificial language. Is Enochian a real glimpse at Heaven's tongue, or, as 17th century scientist Robert Hooke argued, was it a series of codes that Dee used for his intelligence work? Again, answers are not mutually exclusive, as Dee's occultism and intelligence work cannot be separated.[13]

Sadly, during Dee's sojourn in Central Europe in the 1580s, his majestic home in Mortlake, which reputedly contained the largest library in Europe at the time, was ransacked. Many of Dee's priceless books and papers were fed to fires. Such was the double-headed nature of empowering occultists within a Christian kingdom—Dee was as feared as he was respected. Those proud Englishman who cheered his contributions to England's victories over Spain later blamed him for a plague that ravaged the land, claiming Dee's wife and four of his eight children.[14] Dee's final years saw him shunned from the court of King James I (more on him later) because of the Scottish monarch's distaste for occultism and witchcraft. Dee passed away at the old age of eighty-two in

1608. Tragically, the once powerful court magician died alone and in poverty.

Of all of Dee's conjurations, from his sage advice during the Spanish Armada to his many experiments with angels, his most important was his full-throated endorsement of an English Empire across the Atlantic Ocean. Dee's imperial vision first found publication in 1577 with *General & Rare Memorials pertayning to the Perfect Arte of Navigation*. In this book, Dee argued for the English crown to seize power in the New World by first creating a first-class navy (Dee is in many ways one of the intellectual fathers of the large and modern Royal Navy). Dee's book also argues for England's legitimacy as the sole ruler of the New World, thanks to the medieval explorations of the Welsh prince Madog Ab Owain Gwynedd. According to legend, Prince Madog (sometimes called Madoc), left the Kingdom of Gwynedd in northern Wales in the 12th century to undertake a fantastic exploration of the open sea. During this voyage, Prince Madog supposedly found bountiful land somewhere far to the west of Europe. This land, which many today cite as the Southeastern part of the United States, became a home for Welsh settlers. The settlers became so ingrained in their new environment that they intermarried with local tribes, thus forming the nexus of what today are called Welsh Indians.[15] Dee's assertions, which were supported by the Anglican priest and imperialist visionary Richard Haklyut, were meant not only to undercut Spain's claims of sovereignty in the New World, but were also meant to appeal to Queen Elizabeth directly, as she came from the ethnically Welsh House of Tudor.[16] Ultimately, Queen Elizabeth only took up parts of Dee's recommendations in *General & Rare Memorials pertayning to the Perfect Arte of Navigation*.

Rather than enhance the still new Royal Navy, the Queen made do with privateers. Still, the general thrust of Dee's argument, which called for the settling of Englishmen in the New World, went forward, although the first full flowering of this idea occurred under the Queen's successor, James I.

Dee also institutionalized the court-astrologer role in the English kingdom. His figure proved so grand in the English imagination that one of his contemporaries, William Shakespeare, allegedly used Dee as a template for the character of Prospero in *The Tempest*.[17] Dee was also not the last occultist-spy for the English crown, nor would he be the last alchemist and master of the dark arts to pen words in favor of English imperialism.[18] In fact, although King James I banished Dee and other occultists from the court at London, the king himself was a devoted student of demonology. In 1597, while reigning as King James VI of Scotland, the monarch published *Daemonologie*, a treatise that took seriously the threat of witchcraft. James believed sincerely that secret covens of witches used their diabolical powers to undermine the health and vitality of the Kingdom of Scotland, and when he ascended to the English throne, the new King James I quickly passed the Witchcraft Act.[19]

During the Jacobean Age (1603-1625), witchcraft trials and persecutions bloomed in Scotland and England; simultaneously, the English crown expanded its holdings in the New World with settlements at Jamestown (1607), Newfoundland (1610), and Plymouth (1620). Officially, King James's court was anti-occultist. In fact, the new king used the secret service created by his predecessor to hunt down suspected witches. Most notably, King James employed his secret agents to arrest the Earl of Bothwell for allegedly using a coven of Scottish witches to weaken the throne. This proved to be a real departure from the older English model first used by Dee's fellow royal agent, Sir Francis Walsingham, who reportedly employed witches as intelligence agents on the Continent.[20]

The Legacy of British Occultist Imperialism

Shadows of the occult and such practices never left the British Isles. During the English Civil War, witchcraft hunts became a fixture, with the infamous "Witchfinder General" Matthew Hopkins responsible for the execution of some 100 suspected witches between 1644 and 1646. One hundred years later, the Order of the Friars of St. Francis of Wycombe was founded by Sir Francis Dashwood, the future Chancellor of the Exchequer under King George III. This group is better known to history as the infamous Hellfire Club—a debauched society of noblemen that included the American polymath and diplomat Benjamin Franklin. As a young man, Dashwood toured Europe and reportedly joined a Freemason lodge in France. It was also well-known that Dashwood had a deep prejudice against the Roman Catholic Church and an interest in antiquity. These two strands would meet along the River Thames at the headquarters of the Hellfire Club. Not long after the lodge's formation, rumors of orgies and black masses swirled around the group. Gossip-prone Londoners filled their local coffee shops with stories about prostitutes dressed like nuns and other blasphemies. Some of these debaucheries may have occurred. However, according to several sources, the Hellfire Club's primary religious purpose was the revival of the Ancient Greek Eleusinian Mysteries within a British context.[21] Dashwood was likely a closet pagan inspired by the Enlightenment to seek out new religious vistas for the British realm. It is also just as likely that the Hellfire Club engaged in espionage, particularly in the underhanded practice of using blackmail to control the actions of influential people. Not only did the club include several key political figures such as the Lord Mayor of London, Paymaster General Thomas Potter, and John Montagu, the First Lord of the Admiralty, but Dashwood himself engaged in espionage when he spied on the royal court of Russia and on Jacobite agents exiled in Italy.[22] It is also believed that Dashwood and Franklin worked closely on the eve of the American Revolution in order to prevent hostilities from breaking out.

The British Hellfire Club found imitators throughout Europe. Many of these organizations combined intrigue with Satanism and espionage. A century later, during the apex of British power abroad, another occultist began partaking in espionage work. Born Edward Alexander Crowley in 1875 in a spa town in Warwickshire, Aleister Crowley, aka the "Great Beast 666" and the "Wickedest Man in the World," became the occult superstar of the electric age. Crowley matriculated at Trinity College, Cambridge, where he studied the then novel discipline of English Literature. At college, Crowley abandoned his family's Christianity for occult studies. He also changed his name to Aleister and took up his many hobbies, including mountain climbing and chess. Crowley left Trinity College, the former employer of Dee, without graduating. From there, Crowley used his sizable inheritance to live the life of a bon vivant. His first volume of poetry, published in 1898, displayed an obsession with magic, debauchery, and shocking imagery. As a mountaineer, Crowley showed great skill (he took part in two climbs to surmount K2 and Kanchenjunga) and lots of misfortune (four of his fellow climbers died during the Kanchenjunga expedition, and some accused Crowley of ignoring the cries of the doomed men).[23]

But, of all his many endeavors, Crowley is best remembered as a practitioner of magick, especially black and sexual magick. In 1898, Crowley joined the Hermetic Order of the Golden Dawn, a powerful occult society that included such luminaries as weird fiction writer Algernon Blackwood, Sherlock Holmes creator Sir Arthur Conan Doyle, *Dracula* author Bram Stoker, and Irish poet W.B. Yeats. The group, which had ties to equally secretive groups like the Rosicrucians and Freemasons, had as its leader during Crowley's time a mysterious individual by the name of Samuel Liddell MacGregor Mathers. Mathers, a member of the Freemasons, came from a family of Jacobite stalwarts. In the 1890s, Mathers established a Golden Dawn temple in Paris while simultaneously pursuing Jacobite activities, including possible intelligence work. Indeed, under Mathers, the Golden Dawn created a division within the group called the "Secret Chiefs", which Crowley himself compared to an intelligence service.[24] Mathers and the Secret Chiefs oversaw the expansion of the Golden Dawn throughout Europe, thus, by the time Crowley began his revolt within the organization, Golden Dawn lodges could be found in France, the U.K., and Germany.

By 1904, following a religious experience while in Egypt, Crowley composed *The Book of the Law*, a long prose poem supposedly dictated to him by an Egyptian entity called Aiwass. This book became the foundational text for Crowley's new religion, Thelema.[25] Crowley's new occult religion had as its doctrinal slogan, "Do what thou wilt shall be the whole of the law." This philosophical statement, which originated in the 16th century courtesy of French playwright Rabelais's *Gargantua and Pantagruel*, first saw occult use with the Hellfire Club. However, Crowley and his adherents took it much further. Thelema became a secretive yet popular religion among members of the Anglo-American elite. Noticeably, many Thelemites, including those who followed Crowley's to his debased "abbey" in Sicily during the 1920s, had positions of prestige and power within the fields of technology and military science.[26] One of Crowley's British adherents was Major-General John Frederick Charles (J.F.C.) Fuller, the British Empire's chief strategist of armored warfare and one of the earliest supporters of British Fascism. Crowley's most notable American disciple, Jack Parsons, not only helped to found the Jet Propulsion Laboratory, but was also one of the first engineers to successfully design and test a rocket engine. Crowley himself named Parsons as the head of the California branch of the Ordo Templis Orientis (O.T.O.), the primary magical lodge for Thelema.[27]

As for Crowley himself, circumstantial evidence suggests that he enjoyed privileges as a secret agent in the employ of the British government. As noted by author Richard B. Spence, Crowley lived in America during World War I and in Germany prior to World War II. During the Great War, Crowley penned strident pro-German articles, which drew the ire of the American Secret Service. According to Spence, Crowley's pro-German stance was more ruse than reality, as the famous occultist worked as an informer. How else can one explain the fact that the vocally pro-German Crowley continued to live in America after the war, and even had the ear of Henry

Ford during discussions about the proper response to the Bolshevik Revolution?[28] Then, during the interwar period, Crowley spent a great deal of time in Germany. Nominally, he focused on strengthening Thelema and the O.T.O. in the Weimar Republic, where a significant portion of the German intelligentsia had an interest in the occult. Again, Spence sees Crowley's time in Germany as part of a wider operation by London to keep tabs on the extreme political movements within Germany, especially the occult-centered National Socialists. No less of an authority than Ian Fleming recorded that Crowley maintained links with British intelligence during World War II, as the infamous "Great Beast 666" reportedly interviewed Rudolf Hess, himself an ardent student of the occult, following his crash landing in Scotland in 1941.[29] Six years later, in December 1947, Crowley died alone and penniless like his precursor, John Dee.

Occultism and the Intelligence State

We must now turn once again to where we started — the magician State. In a literal sense, the earliest days of the English Empire can be defined as a magician State, with Queen Elizabeth I listening attentively to the ideas and dreams of occultists like Dee and occult-adjacent spies like Walsingham. Elizabeth I's successor, James I, believed in magic and the infernal so much that he used the power of the state to crush suspected witches and their enablers. Tellingly, James I often saw witchcraft as a political tool used by those seeking to dethrone him. Thus, magic and politics have long been closely associated with one another in the English, later British, context. More specifically, there has long existed cooperation between the worlds of occultism and intelligence. Dee, Dashwood, and Crowley likely did both as government agents and practitioners of secret rites. And, if some evidence is to be believed, such individuals and organizations exist to this day.

Following World War II, especially following the intentional destruction of British hegemony during the Cold War, America took up the mantle of the British Empire. As the Third British Empire, or more properly the Third Anglo Empire, the United States today performs many of the same duties as London's old thalassocracy—protection of the sea lanes for international trade, expansion of liberal economic and social ideas abroad, and "policing" restive but economically vital areas like the Middle East and East Asia.[30] Also, it is possible that the United States has succeeded Great Britain as the premiere practitioner of occult-based intelligence work. According to author David McGowan in his book *Programmed to Kill*, there exists disturbing links between the CIA, FBI, and suspected Satanic and pedophilic organizations since at least the 1960s. McGowan's book, which primarily examines the popular myths of serial killers, argues for the notion that the CIA's MKULTRA program, which is a common name for a whole host of programs all designed to study mind control, used occultists and black magick practices, such as the ritualistic abuse of children, to experiment on the American population as a whole. For McGowan, the CIA has "played key roles in the creation of underground satanic cults engaged in violent criminal enterprises," because the MKULTRA experiments taught them that the more people there are who are prone to dissociative states (i.e., people who have suffered chronic abuse, especially as children), the more likely it is to control people through fear.[31] Hence, the creation of a powerful central state within the United States is possible thanks to magic in the form of media manipulation, widespread abuse of the vulnerable, and sensationalist news stories designed to make the citizenry forfeit some of their civil liberties. Such talk has always been considered outlandish and the purview of "conspiracy theorists." Then again, in the wake of COVID-19, which saw an unprecedented centralization of economic power under the guise of protecting public health, more and more Westerners are beginning to see just how manipulative the state can be once it turns the volume on its magical operations up to eleven.

Ultimately, links between magick and the state are well-documented. Great Britain produced warlock-spies like John Dee and Aleister Crowley, who often used their standing as occultists to engage in intelligence gathering or, in Dee's case, international theft. As for the United States, several members of the military-industrial complex, from Jack Parsons to Michael A. Aquino, were active members of various occult groups.[32] Occultism and intelligence work are spiritually related anyway, as both deal in the unknown and in practices of deception, fabrication, and *ad hoc* creation. More bluntly, intelligence work is the work of magick, which John Michael Greer simply defines as: "the art and science of causing changes in consciousness in accordance with will." [33] And, as the post-industrial economy has given way to the so-called "knowledge economy", magick has risen to greater importance within state operations. The control of consciousness has long been the primary focus of the magician State, but now, in anno domini 2022, the magician State often feels itself losing control thanks to the widespread use of a de-centralized Internet. The Internet causes chaos and disruptions within the magician State, and as a result, the current goal of the ruling class is to use their powers of persuasion and force to centralize the Internet. This is the contemporary "psych war", which includes manifold intelligence operations. It is occultism all the way down, from using "Fed" online forum users to creating fake profiles designed to convince dissidents to toe the official line (or push some of the more anti-social personalities past the boundaries of acceptable behavior).

So, while many may snicker at Q-Anon and other such groups who sincerely believe that globalism is the political face of an elite strata who actively engage in Satanism and pedophilia, it can and should never be denied that the modern state engages in occult practices regularly. Often these practices are visible and barely concealed, such as propaganda and media manipulation. Other practices, such as blackmail operations of the kind likely engaged in by billionaire Jeffrey Epstein and Ghislaine Maxwell, are only now coming into focus within the public consciousness. Such operations have existed for a long time—at least since the Elizabethan Age. If they are more prevalent today, it is because the modern magician State requires a greater degree of control over such a complex and interconnected system of politics, entertainment, war, and trade. But the occult practices remain, and the progeny of John Dee have plenty of tricks left to perform.

Endnotes

1. Ioan P. Couliano, *Eros and Magic in the Renaissance* (Chicago: University of Chicago Press, 1987): 105.
2. Ibid, 103.
3. Ibid, 105.
4. John Michael Greer, *The King in Orange: The Magical and Occult Roots of Political Power* (Rochester, Vermont: Inner Traditions, 2021): 98-101.
5. Stone Age Herbalist, *Berserkers, Cannibals & Shamans: Essays in Dissident Anthropology* (Self-published, 2022): 92-93.
6. Nicholas Goodrick-Clarke, *Black Sun: Aryan Cults, Esoteric Nazism, and the Politics of Identity* (London/New York: I.B. Tauris, 2003): 107.
7. University of California, Los Angeles Center for Medieval and Renaissance Studies, Sir Francis Drake Commission, *Sir Francis Drake and the Famous Voyage, 1577-1580* (Berkeley/Los Angeles/London: University of California Press, 1984): 120.
8. Alan Gallay, *Walter Ralegh: Architect of Empire* (New York: Basic Books, 2019): 33.
9. Peter Gentle, "Dr. John Dee – The Original 007," *The World of English*, February 2001, Web.
10. Ibid.
11. Jason Louv, *John Dee and the Empire of Angels: Enochian Magick and the Occult Roots of the Modern World* (Rochester, VT/Toronto: Inner Traditions, 2018): 88.
12. "John Dee: Elizabethan 007, scientist, magician, and spy," *History Extra*, 8 Oct. 2021, Web.
13. Albin Grau, the producer and set designer for the 1922 horror film *Nosferatu*, was a serious student of the occult and belonged to a magical order in Germany. Grau used Enochian symbols in the correspondence between Count Orlok the vampire (played by Max Schreck) and the insane real estate agent Knock (played by Alexander Granach).
14. "John Dee: Elizabethan 007, scientist, magician, and spy."
15. Thanks to the "woke" revolution in American life, the story of Prince Madog and the Welsh Indians has been cast aside as "racist." For adherents to puritanical racial Marxism, the story of Prince Madog is "racist" not only because it undercuts Spanish, and therefore Hispanic, claims to the New World, but it also argues that white Europeans have been on the North American continent for much longer than accepted. For more information on the "woke" perspective, see James Griffiths' article "The racist origins of the myth a Welsh prince beat Columbus to America" published by CNN.com.
16. Dee did not dedicate his book to the Queen, however. Instead, he dedicated it to Sir Christopher Hatton, the Lord Chancellor and the Queen's favorite at court.
17. *The Tempest* is also Shakespeare's only play that deals with the New World. Although technically set on an island in the Mediterranean, *The Tempest* has long been read as a reference to English plantations in the New World, with the savage character of Caliban being a stand-in for the native tribes of America.
18. Glyn Parry, "John Dee and the Elizabethan British Empire in its European Context," *The Historical Journal*, 49, 3 (2006):643-675.

19. Mary Sharatt, "King James I: Demonologist," *Wonders & Marvels*, 14 Apr. 2010, Web.

20. Michael Howard, "The British Occult Secret Service, The Untold Story," *New Dawn* 107 (Mar-Apr. 2008).

21. Sabina Magliocco, *Witching Culture: Folklore and Neo-Paganism in America* (Philadelphia: University of Pennsylvania Press, 2010): 35.

22. Howard, "The British Occult Secret Service."

23. Editors, "Aleister Crowley," *Encyclopedia Britannica*, 8 Oct. 2022, Web.

24. Richard B. Spence, *Secret Agent 666: Aleister Crowley, British Intelligence and the Occult* (Port Townsend, WA: Feral House, 2008): 24.

25. Thelema takes its name from the Greek word for "will."

26. Crowley's Abbey of Thelema did not last long and was forcibly shut down by the government of Benito Mussolini. The reason for this eviction came a year earlier when British disciple Raoul Loveday died from typhoid fever whilst living with Crowley. Following the closure of the abbey, local villagers discovered evidence of black magick rituals and walls decorated with demonic and sexual imagery.

27. Parsons died in a mysterious explosion in 1952. Some consider his death a suicide owing to Parsons's history of depression, as well as being under scrutiny because of his former allegiance to communism. Others have argued for murder, with the motivation being connected to internal warfare within the O.T.O.

28. Spence, *Secret Agent 666*, 166.

29. Micah Hanks, "Ian Fleming, Aleister Crowley, and How the Occultists Won the War," *Seven Ages*, 18 Dec. 2017, Web.

30. The first was the Kingdom of England's many colonial holdings until 1707, followed by the British Empire that came into being after the Acts of Union.

31. David McGowan, *Programmed to Kill: The Politics of Serial Murder* (New York/Lincoln/Shanghai: iUniverse, Inc., 2004): xviii.

32. Aquino joined Anton LaVey's Church of Satan in the late 1960s. Eventually, after refuting many of LaVey's doctrines, Aquino established the Temple of Set in San Francisco in 1975. Throughout this time, Aquino performed his duties as a high-ranking officer in the United States Army. Aquino specialized in psychological warfare, and McGowan indicates in *Programed to Kill* that Aquino was associated with the CIA's infamous Phoenix Program during his two tours of duty in South Vietnam. Aquino and others were accused of ritually abusing children at a daycare center located on the Presidio military base in the 1980s.

33. Greer, *The King in Orange*, 4.

About the Author:

Justin Geoffrey is a Canadian-born but American-raised alchemist, Christian mystic, spiritualist, and writer. He recently published *Full Moon Reaction*, available through Terror House Press.

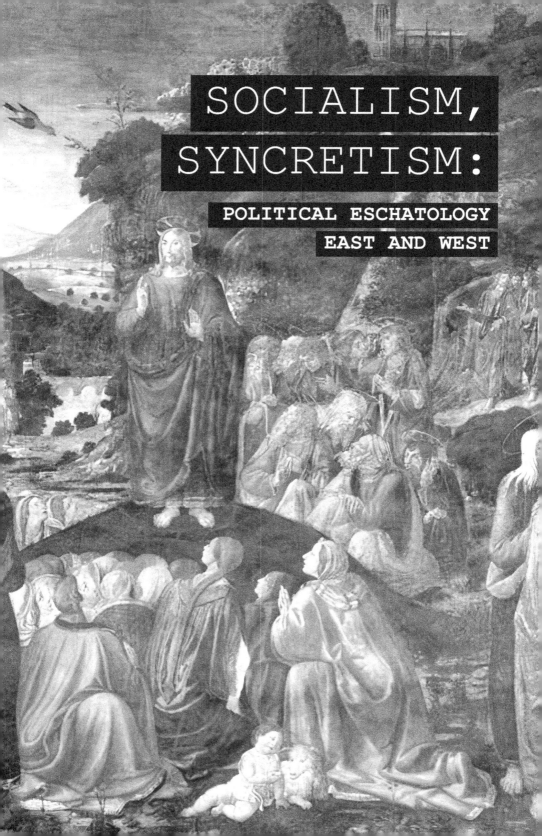

SOCIALISM, SYNCRETISM:

POLITICAL ESCHATOLOGY EAST AND WEST

Socialism, Syncretism: Political Eschatology East and West

By Andrew Cuff

The socialists of the late nineteenth century realized that their ideas would have no staying power or cultural impact unless they took a cue from Christians and began to catechize the youth. They chose perhaps the dullest of all methods: enrolling children in "Socialist Sunday School" (SSS), which for the children was just as wretched as it sounds. A book of socialist hymns and nursery rhymes was made up, containing such gems as a "Hickory, Dickory, Dock" travesty about a little girl oppressed by her money-grubbing factory boss. There were an official socialist Ten Commandments, a socialist *Pilgrim's Progress* about a worker's quest for classless utopia, and a socialist children's magazine (*The Young Socialist*) to communicate directly with the next generation. One issue of this magazine from June 1926 was perturbed by its readers' lack of interest: "I suppose it is because you all have been so excited by the Strike that I have received no solutions for last month's puzzle picture."[1] The SSS eventually went extinct, although its most doltish traditions certainly live on in British and American public schools.

In the twentieth century, the lines between Christianity and socialism were blurred by the "Christian socialist" movements that eschewed Marx-style iconoclasm, preferring to recast genuine Christianity in service of socialist ideology. In both Europe and America, institutions and political organizations of Christian socialists loudly advocated the redistribution of wealth and the end of private property. Communes and brotherhoods were founded, experiments in human nature and utopia to test the ideas of socialist Christians like John Ruskin, Francis Bellamy, and Thomas Hughes. The movement's legacy is present today in seven decades of European Democratic Socialism, and some have drawn parallels between Christian socialism and the social magisterium of twentieth-century Roman Catholicism.

The early socialists' mission has continued to the present day, as modern socialists often herald their political ideology as the only true Christianity. Mikhail Gorbachev claimed in 1992: "Jesus was the first socialist, the first to seek a better life for mankind." [2] Despite the fall of Gorbachev's "utopia", such arguments are common today. For example, Occidental College professor Peter Dreier argued in the *Huffington Post* that "Jesus Was a Socialist" and true Christians must dedicate themselves to fighting big business, stock traders, and especially the "staunch capitalist Donald Trump." As a lifelong Jew, Dreier's "my fellow Christians" appeal is somewhat disingenuous, but that of prominent Eastern Orthodox theologian David Bentley Hart is not: in a series of articles for the *New York Times* and *Commonweal Magazine*, Hart trenchantly rejected any compatibility between Christianity and capitalism. His personal translation of the New Testament for Yale University Press became a part of his argument that socialism literally is Christianity: the principal purpose of both is to condemn all private property (the "old law") and prescribe communal living (the "kingdom of heaven"). American politicians now commonly use Christian scripture and theology to defend election platforms and legislative proposals that are indistinguishable from historical socialism.

A considerable body of literature has nuanced the ostensible syncretism between Christianity and socialism: their shared genre of eschatological historiography, their history of subversive challenge to institutions on behalf of the poor, and their moral rebuke to greed, exploitation, and alienation. Defenses of Christianity rightly denounce the moral missteps of socialism: its totalized state, its rejection of personal ownership, and its denial of fallen human nature. Yet few have mounted a rebuttal that accounts for the radical communitarian metaphysics underlying orthodox Christian social thought. In what follows, we will deploy the resources of premodern Christian theology against socialism's secular eschatology and utopianism, without propping up any of modernity's equally aberrant individualisms.

The fact is, values with a socialist "ring" to them are embedded in the textual tradition and phronema of Christianity. There is a wholesale denunciation of greed and excess riches in writings as early as *Job* and *Proverbs*. Christ's sermon on the mount and his binary division of human beings into moral categories of "the rich" and "the poor" would immediately garner a "radical socialist" label for any modern politician. James, his brother, the first bishop of Jerusalem, wrote polemics that could have been embraced by Friedrich Engels: "Come now, you rich, weep and howl for the miseries that are coming upon you...the wages of the laborers who picked your fields cry out..." (James 5). And the early Christian communities in the *Acts of the Apostles* who "had all things in common" idealized the best of what socialism purports to be.

Many Church Fathers seem to have been friendly to anti-wealth and class-antagonism readings of scripture. Sweeping condemnations of inherited wealth and even commerce, along with declarations that all creation is owned commonly, appear in both Latin and Greek fathers—from Ambrose, Augustine, and Jerome, to Gregory of Nyssa, John Chrysostom, Basil of Caesarea, and Clement of Alexandria. So prevalent are these ideas among patristic sources that an early opponent of socialist theory, Catholic theologian John A. Ryan, felt compelled to publish a lengthy tract in 1913 entitled "Alleged Socialism of the Church Fathers." In it, Ryan makes fine distinctions between types of wealth, calls attention to figurative language, and overall defends private property as a patristic ideal. He also relies heavily on the natural law theory present in Papal Encyclicals on social thought, especially those of Pope Leo XIII.

The question that was obvious to Ryan and others is whether Biblical and early church writings constitute a Christian heritage of socialism, or rather if socialist eisegesis has warped modern readings. Because academics and institutional churches have often approached socialist theory under the influence of political activism, popular opinion, corporate influence, and other factors in the rapidly-changing world of the 20th century, it is very difficult to determine what is socialist and what is socialist-sounding. It can be just as difficult to determine what is Christian and what is Christian-sounding. A close look at how one socialist agitator and professing

Christian answered these questions in the 1960s will reveal just how intertwined the two worldviews had become.

That activist was Dorothy Day, who for her myriad devotees is the "patron saint" of Christian socialism. A convert to Catholicism, Day never lost her exuberance for the confluence between Christian praxis and Socialist ideology, even though she rejected some of its key tenets. Day explained her support for Fidel Castro's socialist revolution in Cuba in an article for her *Catholic Worker* magazine in 1961. While she mourned the anti-religious elements of socialism and communism, Day celebrated their concern for the poor. Ultimately, she supported the regime that persecuted the Catholic Church in Cuba because, in her eyes, it more authentically supported Christianity's mission to the less fortunate. Concluding her defense of the Cuban Revolution, Day paradoxically proclaimed, "God Bless the priests and people of Cuba. God bless Castro and all those who are seeing Christ in the poor." [3]

Dorothy Day here demonstrates the attitude that what is good in socialism and communism can be extracted from what is bad. But are the impulses of socialist thinkers the same as Christ's injunctions to be mindful of the poor? Is it possible to have a Christian socialism that rejects anti-religious elements in the broader movement, but espouses a progressive liberation theology in pursuit of Christ's eschatological promises?

Day, of course, was not the first or last to answer yes. The marriage of Christianity and socialism goes back as far as socialist political philosophy itself. Early Christian socialists affirmed a direct, harmonious link between the two. In 1888, a concerned prelate, the Rev. William J. Cooke, recorded some of his contemporaries' proclamations:

> "As the oak springs from the acorn, so may socialism be traced to Christianity … pure Christianity, as taught by Him Whom men call God and Saviour, leads us inevitably to Communism … the only modern scene where the central ideas are the rights of humanity against scientific arrangements, the raising of the low, the protection of the weak, the abasement of iniquity in high places, and the glorious liberty of this new Gospel preached to the poor."[4]

Rev. Cooke refuted the revisionist history that early Church communal life matched the socialist politics of his day, and reminded his readers that Peter affirmed private property in his rebuke of Ananias.

In the 21st century, the emphasis upon socialism's kindred spirit to Christianity has continued, even if the atrocities committed in the attempt to reify socialism's vision have forced Christians to add caveats. For instance, Bishop Marcelo Sanchez Sorondo, the chancellor of the Pontifical Academy of Social Sciences, declared in 2018 that the Chinese government is the best exemplar of Catholic social teaching. However, attempting to avoid scandal, he assured his fellow Christians that the infamously anti-religious and anti-family government has evolved from its "bad" days during John Paul II's pontificate. Ignoring the oppression and atheism in China, Sorondo highlighted the government's elevation of the common good in contrast to the rampant individualism of the West. To this day the undesirable elements of socialism are, in Christian sympathizers' eyes, non-essential and able to be removed without damage to the whole, its historical catastrophes not-withstanding.

No -isms, no political or philosophical systems, can be isomorphically compared with Christianity. The former are ideological, the latter is spiritual. Every -ism has a sort of origin in either Christianity or some earlier, eventually Christianized belief system like the Hebrew scriptures or pagan myths. But the core belief of socialism, its collectivist optimism, rests on a nostrum about human nature that is fundamentally at odds with Christianity. Indeed, the founding falsehood of socialism is the same antelapsarian state taught in both Judaism and Christianity, the Garden of Eden, where all was shared and there was no scarcity or competition. Then came the fall: but not for socialist progressives. To be sure, some humans behave selfishly, but these miscreants are a bug, not a feature, of the human race. If they can be eliminated, humanity can progress beyond any state of nature or historical period, to a bright future where we return to Eden. This utopia—the anthropological basis of socialism—is not entirely false. It is much the same as the new heaven and new earth described in Christian revelation. However, like the Tower of Babel which tried to reach heaven through human effort, it is doomed in one respect: its humanism.

The doom that awaits all human effort was always a feature of pagan literature. Inevitable fate and the futility of man's works pervades mythological narratives from cultures across the world. The Greeks, both philosophers and poets, asserted time and again that humans could not escape their destinies, that what was written by stars and foretold by oracles would unfailingly come to pass. It was futile not only to try to change an outcome, but to do anything at all: the infernal myths of Sisyphus and his boulder, or the Danaides and their bathtub, starkly depict the doctrine of futility. In the east, an equally ancient tradition emerged among Assyrian cultures, whose belief in the *Irkallu* (an afterlife of eternal torment) was inescapable for all, neither a punishment nor a reward. The Vedic Philosophy which arose in India and swept the Far East taught *Karma*, a moral destiny of inexorable cause and effect, and *Vairagya*, the dispassionate renunciation of desire. Northern European doom was perhaps the most striking: poems like *The Battle of Maldon* and *Beowulf* echo the pervasive sentiment that life's goal and fulfillment was to struggle intensely, but ultimately accept life's futility. As J. R. R. Tolkien wrote in *The Monsters and the Critics*, "[Beowulf] is a man, and that for him and many is sufficient tragedy." [5]

The Judeo-Christian contribution to this univocal human assumption of repetitive futility is the difference between a circle and a slanted line. The circle of history repeats endlessly; man is completely without true agency because his decisions are futile. Some early Greek philosophers like Epicurus identified the shortcomings of a philosophical system without free choice, but never offered a non-deterministic model to replace cyclical time. Consider the ubiquitous symbol of the *orouboros*: the world-serpent shared by Egyptian, Greek, Hindu, and Norse mythology eats his own tail, representing a complete, inescapable loop of history. When Christianity introduced a line, progressing upward to an apocalyptic end of history, it was a philosophical revolution. Human hope springs eternal from change; especially when that change is the design and providence of a personal God.

The Circle and the Line would make a terrible book title, so when the distinguished Renaissance historian C. A.

Patrides wrote about cyclical and linear time, he entitled his treatise *The Phoenix and the Ladder: the Rise and Decline of the Christian View of History*. The phoenix lives its earthly life anew each time it experiences death; the ladder (from Jacob to St. John Climacus) transports humanity to heaven. Patrides' 1960 monograph, which compares pagan philosophy of history to Judeo-Christian, is an inexhaustible treasure-trove of over one hundred texts in chronological order from antiquity to early modernity. With the exception of the *Ecclesiastes* author, whose "vanity of vanities" pessimism Patrides calls "obviously schismatic", there emerges a clear and transformative Hebrew contribution to western cosmology: the providence of God in history, and even more importantly, the promise of His future plan.

Although Patrides stops just short of the period when the philosophy of history became most impactful on world events—that is, the advent of Whig history, Hegelian history, and what C. S. Lewis called "chronological snobbery"—readers of *The Phoenix and the Ladder* are inevitably prompted to ponder the legacy of the circle and the line in our day. When Carl Schmitt argued that theories of the state are secularized theologies, he implied that their prescriptions emerged from their philosophy of history. As St. Paul pointed out, "If there is no resurrection... our preaching is useless." One might as accurately say, "if history is not progressing toward something, our laws and elections and diplomacy are useless."

The political tumult of the modern period, socialist movements especially, are secularized versions of the Christian eschaton. As Eric Voegelin famously explained, history does have an *eidos*, or structure, but the imposition ("immanentization") of such a structure by force is responsible for the turmoil of all modern political ideologies. Rejection of an earthly *eidos*, on the other hand, is fundamental to Christian theological politics, best exemplified in the *Spe Salvi* encyclical of Pope Benedict XVI.

Patrides' historical work was an outgrowth of the political debates among his colleagues. "Dino" declared himself a life-long anti-communist, even if, as a young boy, he had helped the communist-fueled Greek resistance to the Nazi invasion. After his experience with the Greek communists, he left his native country behind for literary studies at Kenyon College under John Crowe Ransom, the southern poet and literary critic who had achieved fame as a founding father of both New Criticism and Agrarianism. During the 1930s, Ransom had spearheaded the Nashville Agrarians' explosive manifesto, *I'll Take My Stand: The South and Agrarian Tradition* (1930). Significantly, the manifesto had begun life under a different title, "Tracts Against Communism." While the Agrarians are primarily known as critics of industrialism, they also saw themselves as defenders of a traditional, Christian, humane life against both the right-wing Hegelian utopianism of technocratic capitalism and the left-wing Hegelian utopianism of communistic socialism.

Both of these modern secularized political theologies represent a desperate, anthropocentric attempt to bring about a promised golden age without the Incarnation. Socialism, both pre- and post-Marx, has inspired countless commune movements since the mid-nineteenth century. These commune movements tried to "hold all things in common" like the early Church, but distorted Christian social teaching into bizarre, experimental micro-societies. For instance, in the pre-Marxist socialist commune of Oneida, New York, members believed that Christ's second coming had already occurred, paving the way for humanity itself to bring about heaven on earth. Sharing all things in common included the overt destruction of the traditional family: the Oneidans practiced free love and raised their children communally in order to actively discourage close parent-child and husband-wife relationships. Most fantastically, these "Christian socialists" believed they could breed away sin and moral weakness, justifying their eugenics experimentations. The heretical eschatology of socialist political theology corrupted its morality.

In the years leading up to the Bolshevik Revolution, Russian novelist Leo Tolstoy was the inspiration behind dozens of these commune groups across the globe. Excommunicated for heresy by the Orthodox Church, Tolstoy preached that Christianity had been misunderstood by centuries of Christians, establishing an institutional church not part of Christ, who in Tolstoy's mind was more of a social justice guru. For Tolstoy, Christ was primarily to be found in the Sermon on the Mount, and not in miracles or in dogma: "The Sermon on the Mount, or the Creed. One cannot believe in both. And Churchmen have chosen the latter."[6]

Locating Christian truth in Christ's social teachings exclusively also impacted Tolstoy's understanding of the Christian view of history. Rather than seek salvation and perfection in heaven, Tolstoy preached perfection on earth through socially-focused good works, rejecting any concept of original sin. At the end of his book, *The Kingdom of Heaven is Within You*, Tolstoy enthusiastically prophesied that the real Christian society would inevitably come, as an ever-more enlightened humanity would see through the corruption, lies, and oppression of millennia:

"So that the prophecy that the time will come when men will be taught of God, will learn war no more, will beat their swords into plowshares and their spears into reaping-hooks, which means, translating it into our language, the fortresses, prisons, barracks, palaces, and churches will remain empty, and all the gibbets and guns and cannons will be left unused, is no longer a dream, but the definite new form of life to which mankind is approaching with ever-increasing rapidity." [7]

Tolstoy removes the Incarnation and Christ's second coming from the history of man's salvation, triumphantly proclaiming, "Men cannot know when the day and the hour of the kingdom of God will come, because its coming depends on themselves alone." [8] The socialist communes that sprang up around his teachings were attempting to immanentize the eschaton, making heaven a place on earth. While these communes might be extreme examples of syncretism, their relocation of the Kingdom of Heaven to here and now is the essence of socialism: nothing more than a gross distortion of the Christian view of history.

But exclusively blaming Marx and other socialist thinkers like Tolstoy for the general impulse of de-Christianized eschatology is historically uninformed. After all, did Christianity not face similarly heretical philosophies of history at its inception? Premillennial chiliasm and Marcionism, both of which have now re-arisen in new modern forms, plagued orthodox theologians until the early fifth century. Arguably, the Christian conception of history was more imperiled in late antiquity than its conception of Trinitarian divinity. The Arians were numerous, educated, and influential—but none of them provoked apocalyptic fear or gnostic antinomianism as did the historiographical heresies.

The medieval church faced a whole catalogue of similar heresies, at first surrounding the millennialist fears of A.D. 1000, and then from the radical poverty movements of the twelfth and thirteenth centuries. Those who have watched Ingmar Bergman's classic *The Seventh Seal* remember how the tumultuous happenings of the high Middle Ages—witchcraft, crusade, plague—contributed to this pandemonium. But some of the foment was also embraced as orthodox reform and integrated by the Church, such as Francis of Assisi's mendicants, officially sanctioned by Pope Innocent III.

However, the most important medieval figure at the center of this movement was not Francis, but one of his precursors, an erstwhile Cistercian abbot named Joachim of Fiore. The twelfth-century ascetic and exegete became widely known for dividing history into three ages: the age of the Father before Christ's incarnation, that of the Son where the Church reigns, and most controversially, the coming age of the Holy Spirit, when the authority of the Church would give way to a "common brotherhood" not unlike Marx's "classless utopia." Joachim featured prominently in Eric Voegelin's *The New Science of Politics* as the medieval thinker who prophesied Voegelin's concept of political eschaton.

Although *New Science* lacked recourse to today's medieval scholarship, and thus mistakes Joachim for a heretical gnostic, its thesis connecting Joachim to the later developments of Hegel and Marx is undeniable. Even in his own day, Joachim's interpreters used his thought as a vehicle for revolutionary movements that sought to redistribute wealth, kill the wealthy, destroy patriarchal and traditional institutions like monarchy and episcopacy, and institute mob rule. Jacobinism, Bolshevism, and Maoism were clearly heralded by such movements, and perhaps by Lutheranism as well, to the extent that Luther's institutional iconoclasm was millenarian and influenced by Joachimism. The fourteenth-century *fraticelli* uprising depicted by Umberto Eco in *The Name of the Rose* looks suspiciously like the Red Brigades terrorizing Italy at the time he wrote.

Whether medieval or modern, progressives have always promised the essentially Christian vision of liberation, particularly for the poor. In their view, liberation can only be accomplished by violently wresting private property from the hands of the wealthy, but bloody revolutions face many obstacles. First, the institutions that serve as the guardians of traditional values and property must be shattered, along with the wealth and political status of those with European ancestry. This is the origin of the commonplace phrase "cultural Marxism." Marxism is political economics, but its ramifications for a culture are encapsulated by what is now called progressivism. Ironically, though Marxism and other types of socialism rely on a Christian intellectual heritage, socialism inevitably subverts Christianity through its attacks on Church, family, and western heritage.

This two-pronged subversion came to the fore when Marx and his critics treated the so-called "agrarian question." Put simply, there was a contradiction within Marxist determinism when it came to agrarian societies that had not fully industrialized. Like factory workers, serfs and other rural laborers were a sort of proletariat, but they were of an entirely different character. Geographic and social factors immunized them to the deleterious cultural effects of urbanization and atomization, rendering them a dangerous reactionary element in the eyes of Marxists. They would impede both capitalism, the destructive force that led to revolution, and the eventual revolution itself. Content to live within their means in traditional modes, the landed peasantry would prove resilient—much like the "doughty" hobbits of J.R.R. Tolkien's Middle-Earth.

But now, as rural populations dwindle and "agrarian" production is just another facet of corporate industry, we are left with a stale false dichotomy between capitalism and socialism. Generations who have suffered from their parents' "Age of Aquarius" now reject the threadbare optimism of both right- and left-wing progressivism. Political optimism and utopianism are giving way to anthropological realism and dogma, even on the left. "Liberals" have become frantic to control human behavior while "conservatives" have given up trying to conserve anything except last decade's liberalism. Twenty-first century man hungers for something deeper: many millennials and their younger successors are turning to tradition, sacrality, authority, and mythology. The prevailing order attacks these illiberal stirrings as "identity politics", or splutters that the younger generations "have forgotten the horrors of the past." But few are listening.

Thus, the battle between socialism and its rivals must be completely reformulated for a twenty-first century audience. Because socialism is a parasite on the Christian order, the only authentic way to answer the rising demand for socialism is to re-establish a Christian order. As Cleanth Brooks noted in his "Plea to the Protestant Churches" in 1936, this will "not necessitate the suppression of the social gospel, though it would involve deciding what sort of social gospel is Christian and what is not. It would not demand cessation of a radical criticism of the present economic order, though it would involve relating that criticism to a positive conception of a Christian society." [9] For conservatives, Brooks' challenge will require deep soul searching: the givens of Enlightenment figures such as Rousseau, Locke, Hobbes, and even Jefferson must be critically re-evaluated, despite their enshrined status as American sacred scripture. This might seem a call to shake the foundations: anti-conservative. However, the truth is that there are no modern foundations to conserve, since modernity is built upon the ruin of the old order; sand, not rock.

What will emerge from the rubble, nobody can predict. There is no antiquarian's chance to reconstitute a past golden age, and nostalgia is no path through the Scylla and Charybdis of individualism and collectivism. Yet this much is evident: as Western Civilization's decadent phase devolves into increasing alienation and animosity, its sufferers will more sharply sense how tired they are of being reduced to unnatural atomization. They will cry out for socialism because it is the only menu option that seems to oppose individualism. Like all heretics, socialists err from an abundance of sincerity, not a lack.

Many oppose socialism by numbering its human casualties or hyperventilating about "bread lines." Memes that mock naïve socialist politicians are funny, but only confirm their supporters' experience of ostracization, disenfranchisement, and alienation. Christians are the only force that can truly combat socialism, because only orthodoxy provides an alternative to modernity. The second coming and eternal reign of Christ is a literal, true eschatology, of which socialism offers just a mirage. To the Christian, socialists are simply heretics:

they have "exchanged the glory of the incorruptible God for an image made to look like mortal man" (Rom. 1:23).

Endnotes

1. *The Young Socialist* (June 1926), Marxists.org.
2. *Daily Telegraph* (June 16, 1992).
3. Day, Dorothy. *On Pilgrimage: The Sixties.* Edited by Robert Ellsberg. Maryknoll, NY: Orbis Books, 2021.
4. Cooke, William J. "Christianity and Socialism" in *Wesleyan Methodist Magazine* (1888).
5. Tolkien, J.R.R. *Beowulf : the monsters and the critics.* London: Oxford University Press, 1963.
6. Tolstoy, Leo. *The Kingdom of God is Within You.* Trans. Constance Garrett. New York: Cassell Publishing Company, 1894.
7. Ibid.
8. Ibid.
9. Brooks, Cleanth. *A Plea to the Protestant Churches.* Boston: Houghton Mifflin, 1936.

About the Author:

Andrew Cuff holds a PhD from Catholic University of America with a focus on medieval intellectual history. He is now the Communications Director for Beck & Stone, a brand consultancy that specializes in serving academic and nonprofit organizations.

Follow him on Twitter: @AndrewJCuff

ORIGINAL TRANSLATION:

JAPANESE PERSPECTIVES
ON THE EAST ASIAN CONFLICT

Editor's Note:

Japanese Perspectives, a duo of essays regarding the Japanese political position on the 1932 Invasion of Manchuria, was originally published in 1933, in the German political science journal Zeitschrift für Politik. Despite the nationality of its authors, it was originally penned in German, specifically for a European audience. We present it here not necessarily as an endorsement of what it says, or as a vindication of Japanese actions during WWII, but rather as insight into a historical perspective that one does not often encounter on its own terms: that is, a sympathetic view of Japanese imperialism.

Japanese Perspectives on the East Asian Conflict

Toyowo Ohgushi & T. Takashima

Translated by Shocco

"Three Remarks on the Manchurian Question"
by Toyowo Ohgushi

I. There is an inherent misconception in Europe regarding Manchuria, in that it is historically and popularly a part of China. In contrast, the following quote from the Chinese professor Carsun Chang, the former president of the Institute for Politics in Woosung (Shanghai), from the annual book of public law, volume 19, 1931, p. 318, quote:

> "The Manchu tribes originally lived in northern Manchuria. In 1583 their leader, Nurhachu,[1] conquered all of Manchuria and expanded his influence into Mongolia and Korea. In 1644, the Manchus under their leader Turgon invaded Beijing, made it their capital and founded the Qing dynasty. The Chinese viewed the Manchus as barbarians and hated their rule. They felt it was a particular shame that they had to change their clothes and wear a pigtail. They also regarded it as a disgraceful state of affairs that Manchu

garrisons were stationed in all provinces and that the ministries were initially only occupied by Manchus, later by both Manchu and Chinese. Although the Manchus had adapted to the Chinese in language and way of life over the course of more than two centuries, the gulf between the two peoples remained unbridgeable."

This quote will suffice to establish the correctness of my assertion. But the importance of the Great Wall, which is known to have been built to protect the Chinese against incursions by "barbarian peoples", must also be added. The Great Wall is the demarcation of central China from foreign countries, including Manchuria.

II. In the 1931 issue [2] of the Zeitschrift für Politik, Volume 21, p. 582, Dr. Hsu Dau-lin writes in the article "Japanese Continental Policy and the Problem of Railway Policy in Manchuria":

"To this end, China is planning to expand the port of Hulutao not far from the mouth of the Liao. Then the goods to be transported from Manchuria, no matter where they come from, will no longer be routed via Mukden to the Japanese port of Dairen,[3] but will be shipped either via Mukden or via Dahushan to the Chinese port of Hulutao; that's the death-blow for Dairen..." "This is undoubtedly one of the decisive reasons for Japan's warlike actions in China, all the more so since the Japanese had the Dunghua-Huining line built within the first few days after their invasion of Mukden, and further had completely destroyed the Mukden Bypass Railway Station, the largest station in China, and the uncompleted structure of Hulutao Port."

It is Mr. Hsu Dau-lin's fairytale idea that the Japanese, striving for economic advancement in Manchuria, destroyed the Mukden Bypass Railway Station and Hulutao Port. Both the station and the port are, at least for the moment, under Japanese occupation. Why should the Japanese destroy these important economic institutions? Visible evidence to the contrary of the assertions from Dr. Hsu Dau-lin is in front of me, namely a picture—which I put at the disposal of the editors of the magazine for politics—of the port of Hulutao. It was taken just after the port was occupied on January 4, 1932. General Changhsuliang[4] had the port, which, according to Mr. Hsu Dau-lin's description, meant the "death blow" for the Japanese port of Dairen in the future, expanded as secretly as possible; observation of the port was strictly forbidden. The expansion was in the hands of a Dutch engineer, but what a surprise for the Japanese when, upon occupation, they found that the work had got stuck at the very beginning. There is only one primitive mole[5] there, which no modern ship can dock at. Japan therefore had no reason to destroy this hardly usable facility.

III. The Manchu conflict has now been illuminated from all sides, and many factual treatises are available. But the material is less important than the method of dealing with the topic. Based on this thought, two points should be mentioned that are missing in almost all the literature that I have looked at:

1. The historical treatment of the Manchurian conflict. It usually begins either with the Treaty of Shimonoseki[6] or a few years earlier with the events in Formosa,[7] which are said to be the starting points of modern Japanese expansionism. But the foreign policy of a state can never be understood

without considering its relationship to the other powers in the world. Thus, modern Japanese foreign policy is only overlooked in connection with the actions of the great powers in East Asia, which began early on the part of England, France and Russia—just think of the Opium War in China in 1839. In contrast, Japan only gained a foothold on the East Asian continent in 1905 with the Russo-Japanese War and in 1910 with the annexation of Korea. Thus, Japanese expansion on the continent belongs to a later phase in history than the incursion of the great powers into China. The fact that Japan was not able to consolidate its power on the continent immediately after its victory over China in 1895, but only after the Russo-Japanese War, clearly shows that the so-called Japanese expansion of power was nothing other than a fight against the actions of the already resident great powers. This also explains why Japan directed its power north rather than south—which is inherently more favorable for the emigrating, climate-sensitive Japanese; the more suitable Japanese line of extension runs to the southwest, as Adolf Grabowsky correctly explains in his essay "Die Konstruktion des euasischen Raums" [8] (Leipzig 1932, C.L. Hirschfeld). But the fact that this line is already blocked beyond Formosa can be explained by the expansion movements of the great powers. The historical treatment of the Manchurian conflict should therefore always be done in connection with the international situation, which has only been hinted at here.

2. In order to clarify the meaning of the Manchurian conflict, some special tendency is usually assumed, for example, there is talk of Japanese efforts to dominate the great

powers in East Asia or of a Japanese imperialist struggle against the Bolshevik threat, one even hears of a Japanese-French alliance in opposition to the Anglo-Saxons, etc. All these points of view allow only a one-sided perspective. It should not be forgotten that the Manchurian conflict is of eminent world history importance and that it brought a completely new picture to the international situation of the post-war epoch. However, the conflict must not yet be seen in overly concrete outlines. It is by no means finished, but is still in the middle of development.

"The Source of Error in the Assessment of the Sino-Japanese Conflict" by T. Takashima

The numerous, completely distorting reports about the last Sino-Japanese conflict remind me vividly of the press releases about Germany in Japan at the beginning of the world war. Although many Japanese were familiar with Germany through personal visits and although they sympathized with it, these reports, written purely for propaganda purposes, undermined belief in the integrity of German diplomacy and the chivalry of the German soldier. Regarding this atmosphere, Count Carlo Sforza wrote two interesting articles on this problem in the Vossische Zeitung on February 28 and March 2, 1932. Precisely because Sforza was personally acquainted with the conditions in the Far East and because, as a well-known pacifist, he was supposed to take a neutral standpoint, I feel obliged to add a few more facts in order to facilitate a correct assessment of the situation, all the more so since the Japanese side has so far been patiently hesitant with the expressions of opinion in the German press.

It is highly understandable when Count Sforza warns against attempting to judge the development of Asian events with the pitiful logic of Western mentality. What is the source of the error? No one will deny that the conflict has revealed that China must not be viewed as a unified state, either internally or externally. This had to be taken into account in all future international negotiations.

China doesn't even have a unified currency, so one must face trouble after trouble when traveling in China. There is a common language "Kwanhoa"; [9] but this "official" language is understood by at most one million of the four hundred million inhabitants. The provincial dialects are also different. There is a general lack of a unified feeling and a unified national consciousness; the population of the canton province in 1894/95 for example, didn't even know that China was at war with Japan. The examples of this inner conflict could be multiplied at will, but it is unnecessary, since numerous pro-China descriptions, yes, even declarations from the Chinese side themselves tend to give this away.

One speaks of the Japanese Empire and the Chinese Republic. If one wanted to deduce from this that Japan was imperialist and China was republican, one would make a huge mistake. The current Chinese central government is purely a general dictatorship that takes no account of the interests of the entire population; this is evident even from the indictment of the Chinese delegate in Geneva, Dr. Yen, in which he confirmed that 20,000 Japanese soldiers conquered all of Manchuria, including a population of 40 million Chinese, in a few months. How something like this should be possible if this population were anti-Japanese, or if they had even the slightest feeling of gratitude towards the Chinese ruler there or the Chinese central government, is absolutely incomprehensible.

As far as Japanese "imperialism" is concerned, Count Sforza rightly emphasizes that no people have understood the economic futility of wars—even in victory—as well as the Japanese, and that the Japanese wanted to have peace and friendly development of their relations with China. But he is wrong in that he attributes this deep democratic trend in Japan to a "transformation" and speaks of the steadfast devotion to the mikado[10] and bushido as if these ideas ran counter to the idea of democracy; even the modern Japanese state had no meaning and no possibility of existence without the intimate relationship between the dynasty and the population. The modern Japanese state is essentially the same state as when the empire was founded three thousand years ago, and the spirit from which it was born and by which it lives is that of genuine and true democracy, which is found in bushido and in the deepest communion between the dynasty and the population.[11]

I also cannot agree with Count Sforza's conviction that the Japanese people were, if not during the present conflict, at least in the war of 1904,[12] aggressive and enthusiastic about war. The population of Japan is far too reserved, too peaceful and too understanding to be able to be incited against innocent foreign populations with agitation. During the sending of troops, including those to Tsingtao[13] in 1914 and to Siberia in 1918, in accordance with the conventions of the allied powers, not the slightest trace of hatred towards the nationals of the enemy states could be detected, and it may well be known how friendly the Japanese were towards prisoners.

But what has happened now to inspire the peaceful people of the dreamy cherry blossoms that they throw their own fate into the fire for honor and existence?

Count Sforza's assertion regarding the statistics of immigration to Manchuria over the last twenty years is correct in so far as the number of Japanese has increased by less than 200,000, while that of the Chinese has increased by millions, clear evidence of impeccable Japanese administration. The failure of Japanese immigration now has a special reason. It is true that Manchuria is so primitive that it presents considerable difficulties to the civilized Japanese, but a period of twenty years is not too short for the Japanese to raise Manchuria to a highly civilized country, to the benefit not only of the Chinese and Japanese, but also to the benefit of all other civilized nations, provided that the Japanese had been able to exercise the rights accorded them by treaty with the Chinese government. However, the Chinese government has systematically violated these treaties, it has undermined and annihilated every cultural activity, it has robbed the innocent Chinese of all their belongings, it has threatened those who wish to do business with Japan with the death penalty. Notwithstanding all the long-suffering with which Japanese diplomacy tried to obtain observance of the concluded treaties by negotiation, secret intrigues continued defiantly and intensified; vigorous propaganda was even launched in the Chinese elementary schools to educate the harmless school-children to be anti-Japanese, and parallel to this new propaganda direct acts of violence against the Japanese were perpetrated everywhere in Manchuria and throughout China. The firm and clear line of the policy of reconciliation that Japan has adhered to for more than ten years, which has unswervingly pursued the goal of maintaining friendship with the Chinese government and amicably resolving any differences, no matter how long the road, is with met with constant resentment and with constant insults to Japan. How is it possible to carry out peaceful construction work in the service of civilization if communication with the inhabitants of the contractually guaranteed area is indirectly prevented and no security whatsoever is guaranteed for the future? Since there is not yet a supranational executive power, a state has only one means left to save its nationals from danger, namely to defend itself against violence, even with violence, in the exercise of a sacred and internationally recognized right of sovereign states, the right of self-defense.

If the scheming Nanking government is to be hit; it should be forced to keep contracts, it should be prevented from committing breaches of contract. In no way is Japan's defense directed against the Chinese population, who are rather happy when Japanese troops invade, because they are protected from the plundering of the soldiers and the robbery of the bandits without having to give any contribution or compulsory tax. So both the assumptions and the results are incorrect when Count Sforza writes that imperialist Japan is about to shoot its customers dead.

After realizing that efforts with the Chinese government are futile, Japan tries the new way: directly with the Chinese people, a free and hardworking, peace-loving people of four hundred million; attempting to achieve friendly, neighborly relations in common work towards the ideal of the peaceful advancement of civilization, the goal to which Count Sforza in good faith urges Japan.

So much for Manchuria. In Shanghai things are different. Japanese state policy and the policy of the Japanese people under the leadership of their genrōs[14] cannot be compared with the policy of Chinese governments; Japan knows what interests the great powers have in Shanghai, and Japan respects and honors them. But here, too, the urgent need for self-defense required intervention regardless of all misgivings, not only because of the persecution of Japanese nationals there, but also because of secret Bolshevik propaganda and communist action being carried out there, which is aimed directly at the Japanese state and its secret headquarters, apparently in Shanghai. The assassin who threw a bomb against the Emperor on January 8, 1932[15] had his thoughts poured into Shanghai, and the Chinese troops, especially the lower officer circles in Shanghai, are strongly Bolshevik. Actions by Japan in this direction not only defends the country itself, but also the cultural assets of all mankind.

It is very unfortunate that these circumstances are so little known and that unscrupulous Chinese propaganda with fantastic claims has often found its way into the European press and has created completely wrong ideas. As things stand, intervention by third parties can have no other result than creating intolerable complications, and it seems as if the League of Nations is once again adopting this view.

It is not to be feared that the interests of the Chinese population and the members of the civilized powers will in the future be less favorable than hitherto as a result of the independence of Manchuria and the actions of the Japanese in Shanghai; on the contrary, Japan hopes that with her struggle she will make a sacrifice for the development of civilization and for the freedom of peace for all civilized mankind.

Endnotes

1. Nurhaci, a Jurchen chieftain whose descendants would later go on to found the Qing dynasty.
2. Ohgushi is slightly mistaken—the article he's quoting from is from the 1932 issue—but all the other information is correct.
3. Currently Dalian, PRC. Was called Dalniy in Russian, but the Japanese took the city after the Russo-Japanese War and called it Dairen.
4. Chang Huseh-liang, the Young Marshal.
5. A pier mole.
6. Treaty of Shimonoseki, the treaty that ended the First Sino-Japanese War.
7. The Republic of Formosa and events surrounding it.
8. I've retained the native title here for Grabowsky's essay, but its meaning is "The Construction of the Eurasian Space."
9. I believe this is a romanization of guóyǔ (国语/國語) which apparently means "national language."
10. 御門, literally meaning "the honorable gate" referring to the gate of the Japanese Imperial Palace, is used here to refer to the Emperor.
11. I took the liberty of editing these two sentences, as in the original it was one long, run-on sentence that wouldn't flow well in English.
12. The Russo-Japanese War.
13. Qingdao, PRC.
14. Genrō (元老).
15. I believe the Sakuradamon Incident.

Shocco is a translator and writer who mostly works with German and French literature. You can find his work at Shocco.carrd.co.

Follow Shocco on Twitter: @shoccolotto

Thank you for reading The Dissident Review.

Follow us on Twitter: @Dissident_Rev

For more articles, information, & to submit your writing, our website is www.dissidentreview.com

Made in the USA
Middletown, DE
19 July 2023

35461659R00099